advent

THE WEARY WORLD REJOICES

LIFEWAY WOMEN

Lifeway Press® Brentwood, Tennessee

Published by Lifeway Press®
© 2023 Lifeway Christian Resources • Brentwood, TN

ISBN: 978-1-4300-8844-8 • Item: 005846515
Dewey decimal classification: 263.91
Subject headings: ADVENT / CHRISTMAS / JESUS CHRIST —
NATIVITY

To order additional copies of this resource, write Lifeway
Resources Customer Service; 200 Powell Place, Suite 100,
Brentwood, TN 37027-7707; FAX order to 615.251.5933; call toll-
free 800.458.2772; email orderentry@lifeway.com; or order online
at lifeway.com.

Printed in the United States of America

Lifeway Women Bible Studies
Lifeway Resources
200 Powell Place, Suite 100,
Brentwood, TN 37027-7707

Cover photo by © Ace & Whim

EDITORIAL TEAM,
ADULT MINISTRY
PUBLISHING

Faith Whatley
Director, Adult Ministry

Michelle Hicks
Manager, Adult Ministry
Short Term Bible Studies

Emily Chadwell
Content Editor

Lindsey Bush
Production Editor

Lauren Ervin
Graphic Designer

Chelsea Waack
Cover Design

CONTENTS

HOW TO USE THIS STUDY

Welcome! This Advent study may vary from others you've done. We know many Bible study groups don't meet during the Advent season, so we wanted to provide a study you can do alone, with family, or with your friends! Along with daily personal study, we provided activities each week you may choose to do by yourself, with your kids, or with friends. Each week you'll find:

- an introduction;
- five days of personal study;
- activities to do individually, with kids and teens, or with your friends and family;
- group discussion questions in the Group Guide.

Use the five days of personal study to reflect, allowing God's Word and truth to nourish your soul. This study is designed to help you remember the hope, peace, joy, and love of Jesus during the Christmas season.

GROUP DISCUSSION

If you decide to do this study with others, use the Group Guide discussion questions and the personal study each week to guide your conversation. In addition to answering the questions in the Group Guide, invite women to share the things they learned from each day or to share Scripture and anything that really impacted them during the week. During a group meeting you may want to invite women to share how they've incorporated the kids, teens, and adult activities into the season of Advent. If you choose, your group may want to bring the supplies needed and do one of the activities in a group setting as you discuss the Group Guide questions and personal study.

Because Advent can be a busy season, we hope the activities in the study provide a time of rest and reflection. We hope you'll enjoy sharing the love of Jesus with your family, friends, and neighbors this season.

A GROUP TIME MIGHT LOOK SOMETHING LIKE THIS:

- Welcome (This might also be a time to light a candle if you choose to include an Advent wreath each week.)
- Ask the questions on the Group Guide page for that week.
- Review the five days of personal study.
- Ask women to share any special activities they added to their week as they focused on Advent.
- Read Scripture related to the week's theme (hope, peace, joy, love). You can find a list of Scriptures for each week of Advent on page 142.
- Close in prayer.

SHARE WITH OTHERS

There may be those in your neighborhood or community who don't understand Advent. Consider inviting others to join you, using the Group Guide questions and hosting a group in your home. Explain the Advent wreath, what the Bible says about Jesus, and how your celebration of the Christmas season is different because of Christ.

INTRODUCTION

We want to celebrate the birth of Christ. We know it's important to remember the "reason for the season," both in our hearts and in our actions. But perhaps Christmas has lost a bit of its wonder and beauty. It can be easy to look at gift giving as an obligation, and our calendars become so full of parties and concerts and entertaining that we wonder if we'll have a moment to breathe. We struggle to remember why we're doing all of this. What are we celebrating? How can we keep our focus on Christ, the One whose birth and love we celebrate this season?

We hope this study will help. Advent may not be a word you're used to using when it comes to this season. Advent, by definition, means "the arrival." During Advent, we remember what it was like to wait for Jesus' first Advent on earth—Christmas.

Advent, officially, is a season on the church calendar leading up to Christmas. Traditionally, it begins the fourth Sunday before Christmas and goes until Christmas day. The rituals and traditions associated with Advent are both ancient and fluid. Churches have observed Advent for centuries, but each congregation and individual may participate in different ways. Many light candles each Sunday, telling a different part of the Christmas story leading up to Christ's birth. We've included a quick guide for you on page 142.

Advent is important in many ways. Here are some you might consider.

ADVENT CHALLENGES US TO FOCUS ON JESUS IN THE WEEKS LEADING UP TO CHRISTMAS.

Amidst the hustle and bustle and jingle bells, taking time to observe Advent invites us to remember the hope, peace, joy, and love Jesus offers. We are challenged to keep the other holiday festivities centered on who Jesus is and what His coming means for us.

ADVENT BUILDS ANTICIPATION.

When we think and read about the prophets predicting Jesus' birth, it makes us thankful for the hope of Jesus. When we're reminded of the Israelites enslaved and then in exile, we become grateful for the God who is with us—Immanuel. We anticipate celebrating Jesus' first coming, but Advent also points us to His second. We still long for hope, for peace, for joy, for God With Us. In Jesus' second coming, we will have perfect hope, peace, joy, and love, and we will be with God for eternity.

Different churches tell the story in different ways. We've chosen to focus on an attribute of Jesus' coming each week, along with someone in the Christmas story. The first week, we'll talk about the prophets who foretold Jesus' birth with hope. The second week, we'll look at how the angels declared peace had come to earth. The third week, we'll talk about the joy of the shepherds. Finally, on Christmas week, we'll celebrate the love of Christ Himself.

Advent helps remind us, as the familiar Christmas carol says, of when "He appeared, and the soul felt its worth." We pray as you study the story of Immanuel this Advent season, that your soul will feel its worth—that you will be filled with the hope, peace, joy, and love of Christ. We pray this Christmas you'll remember that one holy night long ago with gratitude and wonder and look forward to the second Advent when Christ returns victorious.

HOPE

WEEK 1

THE WEARY WORLD

by Elizabeth Hyndman

The subtitle for this study on Advent most likely sounds familiar to you. We borrowed the line from one of our favorite Christmas hymns, "O Holy Night!" The full line sings, "A thrill of hope—the weary world rejoices."[1]

Today, we identify with the last part of that line, even though it was written in 1847 and translated into English in 1855.[2] The truth is, our world has been weary since Genesis 3. You feel it. I feel it. The writers of the hymn and the writers of the Old Testament felt it. We're weary of the darkness, the pain, the doubt, the fear. We stand waiting.

The writers of the Old Testament knew, though, that the wait would not last forever. Even in the midst of waiting, the thrill of hope sustained them. They could rejoice because they trusted in their hope of a promise—the promise of the Messiah, the Light of the world.

They waited with hope. The weary world waited while brothers killed one another, while men walked on the earth for hundreds of years, while generation after generation died. They waited as they witnessed the entire earth covered in water, wiping out every living creature except a handful of the faithful. They waited, however impatiently, while trying to take matters into their own hands— they attempted to become their own saviors, building towers into heaven.

The world nodded along hearing a promise tinged with familiarity as God vowed to make Abraham into a great nation. Our forefathers waited as they obeyed God's commands to go to unfamiliar lands. They waited through famine, through slavery, through wandering, through wars.

While the wars raged and seemed never-ending, God's people looked to heaven and asked, "How long? How long must we wait for your promise to be fulfilled?" God granted them kings in their waiting, pointing to the King who was coming. He gave words to their prophets, promising again and again: the Light will come.

And they waited. They waited as the darkness grew, as the light seemed to flicker out. They waited in darkness, in silence.

And they hoped.

Here and now, we stand waiting and hoping as well. We stand on the other side of the time line. We look back at the first Advent, toward the second one. We are waiting on the Messiah to return, to defeat the enemy, to drive back the darkness once and for all. We are waiting for all things to be made new. We are waiting on the hope of the promise to be fulfilled.

We have the privilege of knowing the full story. We know the promised Messiah came to earth, He died for the sins of the world, and He is risen, conquering death and darkness, pain, doubt, and fear. He is our "thrill of hope." He is the reason this "weary world rejoices."

What's your favorite Christmas tradition?

Are you familiar with Advent? Did you celebrate Advent growing up? Do you celebrate it now?

During Advent we remember how God's people waited for the promise of the coming Messiah. When have you experienced a long season of waiting? What emotions did you feel during that time? Anticipation? Impatience?

Proverbs 13:12 says, "Hope deferred makes the heart sick" (NIV). Describe a time when your hope was deferred. What did God teach you through that experience?

Close your time with prayer, asking God to prepare your heart for the season of Advent. Pray for those who are in a painful season of waiting, that God would renew their hope and faith in Him.

WAITING WITH HOPE

by Sarah Doss

First, read Genesis 3.

As we dive into our study of Advent, we need to understand the *why* behind it all—the reason Jesus came to earth to save us.

> Though Genesis 3 includes a story that is likely familiar to you, take a few moments to consider the passage anew. Write at least one insight you glean in the space provided below.

Adam and Eve entered into a perfect world. They had an intimate relationship with God and a harmonious relationship with one another—no strife, no miscommunication, no competition or judgment. (Doesn't that sound nice?) But, as we know, this wholeness—this perfect communion with God and one another—was shattered by an act of disobedience on the part of Adam and Eve. They ate of the tree of the knowledge of good and evil, in effect telling God that they thought they knew better than He did. And, we know now, this act of disobedience would forever change the nature of humanity, as each of us inherits a sin nature from Adam and Eve. We are born separated from God because of our sin. Our innate desire is to go our own way and to live contrary to God.

> Let's focus for a few minutes on Genesis 3:14-15. What do you think verse 15 means?

The serpent's judgment would involve defeat by the woman's offspring. In His pronouncement of judgment on Adam, Eve, and the serpent, God showed grace to Adam and Eve in promising them a way to defeat the serpent and a way to be restored to right relationship with Him, which was the biggest grace of all.

In Genesis 4:1, we find the account of the first human birth in the history of humanity. Though it's such a small, matter-of-fact mention, can you imagine what might have been going through Adam and Eve's minds as she was laboring and eventually gave birth? It's nerve-wracking enough to be a first-time mom, let alone the first person in the history of the world to give birth. But surely their joy and wonder overshadowed those fears. Scholar James Boice says Adam and Eve likely thought Cain was the deliverer who would defeat the serpent that God promised in Genesis 3:15. It's even reflected in the name they gave him.[3] Boice says, "In view of the promise of a deliverer, [Cain's] name probably means 'Here he is' or 'I've gotten him.' Eve called her son 'Here he is' because she thought the deliverer had been sent by God."[4]

Adam and Eve thought their deliverance was coming soon, but Cain wasn't the deliverer. Instead, he seemed to be a tortured soul who murdered his brother and walked in disobedience to God all of his days. I wonder how disappointed Adam and Eve were to realize their deliverance wasn't coming through Cain; their hope was deferred. Adam and Eve had no idea what their deliverance would look like, but there was still hope in God's promise.

That thread of hope continued throughout the Old Testament as God sent prophecies of the coming Deliverer—Jesus, who would ultimately defeat Satan, sin, and death in His sacrifice on the cross and His resurrection three days later. For years and years, people lived in anticipation, trusting that God would send their Deliverer, waiting for every new glimpse of hope as God revealed more about who the Deliverer would be and when He would come.

That's where we find ourselves in this season of Advent. Though we are on this side of Jesus' ministry on earth, during Advent we spend intentional time considering the years of waiting that God's people endured in the Old Testament, and we allow it to fuel our praise and gratitude for Jesus' coming.

> Take a moment to write a short prayer of praise to God for Jesus' coming to earth to rescue us and to give us a right relationship with Him.

We also take time during Advent to consider our own seasons of waiting. We are still waiting for the Savior's ultimate return, waiting for the fulfillment of His kingdom on earth. We're in the already but not yet. We've been given a taste of the kingdom of God, as we see seeds of redemption sown on the earth, as we are taught and led in sanctification by the Holy Spirit, as people come to a saving knowledge of Christ, and as God teaches us to love one another. But, in a very real sense, we are still waiting for the final redemption of all things.

Read Romans 8:18-25. Below, write a paraphrase of each verse in your own words.	
verse 18	
verse 19	
verse 20	
verse 21	
verse 22	
verse 23	
verse 24	
verse 25	

Which of these verses was encouraging to you? Explain.

WE, ALONG WITH ALL OF CREATION, ARE STILL GROANING, LOOKING IN HOPE TO OUR SAVIOR, LOOKING IN HOPE TOWARD THE DAY WHEN HE WILL COME AND MAKE ALL THINGS NEW AND GOD WILL BE GIVEN THE GLORY HE IS DUE.

We are waiting for Christ's second return, and we are also waiting on specific things in our lives.

Are you waiting on the Lord for something in particular? It can be something small or big, a longstanding hope and desire or a fly-by-night prayer. Describe the situation below.

When you consider the waiting that God's people endured for centuries, does it help you in your waiting? Or make it harder? Explain.

We all have hopes and desires that seem unfulfilled now. Everyone is waiting for something. It can be hard to perceive God's love and care for us when we aren't always able to see His work in our lives. It's difficult to live in the tension of knowing God's love for us and what looks to us at times to be His inactivity in our waiting or suffering. The people of God have bumped up against this reality for centuries; in fact, God gives us many biblical texts, especially the Psalms, to show us how to dialogue with Him in these moments of seeming incongruity.

I love what A. W. Pink says about seasons when we're not sure what exactly God is doing in our lives:

> Though you cannot now harmonize God's mysterious dealings with the avowals of His love, wait on Him for more light. In His own good time He will make it plain to you.[5]

In seasons of waiting, even if you can't see it, God is working on your behalf. He is forming you into His image. He loves you, and He wants you to know Him more intimately. Though it's challenging, let's allow these seasons of waiting to strengthen our faith and fuel our hope in the coming Savior.

Take a few minutes to journal a prayer to God about something you're waiting on Him to answer. Tell Him about the places where your faith feels frail and ask Him to strengthen it. Praise Him for His faithfulness, how He cares for you, and how He's coming back to make all things new.

HOPING IN THE UNEXPECTED

by Ashley Marivittori Gorman

First, read Isaiah 55:8.

"May the odds be ever in your favor."

Anyone familiar with *The Hunger Games* cringes at this phrase. After all, everything about the games was designed for the powerful (the Capitol led by President Snow) to watch the powerless (the districts) fight for their lives in the goriest of circumstances, only to fail and remain oppressed.

To wish the tributes well was cruel—everyone knew the odds were most certainly *not* in anyone's favor. Only one person could come out of the games victorious, and if you were chosen to go in, odds were, the victor wouldn't be you. No one wanted to be willingly subjected to that kind of torture. Unless, of course, love was part of the equation.

In a suspenseful moment, a frail little girl named Primrose was chosen to compete, and everyone fell silent in horror. As Primrose made her way forward, like a lamb led to the slaughter, her sister, Katniss, full of rage and compassion and love, unexpectedly screamed a sacrificial phrase—"I volunteer as tribute!" Someone was going to have to be sacrificed, and Katniss willingly stepped on the altar for the sake of her sister.

Though Primrose and Katniss were similar in some ways, Primrose was young, and her perspective on the games was limited compared to Katniss' experience. She assumed her only option was to simply go along with the current order of things. She couldn't see another way, so she walked toward her doom. But Katniss was older, wiser, and more skilled; she had a different take on the situation. She knew there was another way to satisfy what was required while also sparing Primrose. And, as unexpected as it was, she moved on it.

When we look at Isaiah 55:8, we see a similar idea. Though being made in God's image makes us like Him in many ways, this verse helps us see that we aren't *just* like Him. For example, His thoughts aren't like ours, and His ways aren't like ours either. They are different. They are higher. Where we have partial or limited information in any given situation, God has complete understanding and is always working with the full scope of the facts. He knows what we don't know. He sees what we can't see. He takes into account things we never knew were there. He's infinitely "older and wiser" than us. When He deals with any given problem, He usually approaches it in a totally different way than we would.

How has Jesus worked in unexpected ways in your life? Be specific.

In what situations in your life are you trusting that your ways are better than God's?

In what area of your life have you forgotten that the God you serve is the God of the unexpected? How can you remind yourself of this truth?

What unwelcome or unexpected circumstances do you need to surrender to God fully, trusting that His ways are higher?

When things don't go according to your plan, how do you react? How can you adjust your responses to align with Isaiah 55:8?

In the incarnation, God solved a cosmic problem—humanity's separation from Him—in a completely different way than we would. Where we naturally started walking toward our doom—whether that be by working harder, or strategizing some sort of compromise, or throwing out the idea of sin altogether—God didn't do any of that. He knew that working harder would not bring us back to Him. He knew that compromise wasn't an option. He knew that pretending like sin didn't exist wasn't going to work either. We were walking toward our slaughter, but God knew a way to satisfy what was required for our sin while still sparing us. And, unexpected as it was, He moved on it.

And what was that unexpected way? God offered His Son as tribute. As His prodigal children trudged their way into the horrors of paying for their own sin, Jesus made His way forward, compelled by His compassion and love and rage against sin, and He took our place.

But here's where the analogy breaks down. In *The Hunger Games*, Primrose didn't deserve the fate she was walking toward. In our case, we do. Though we all want to be the innocent little sister in the picture, the truth is that we are the Capitol—guilty, corrupt, and compromised by the fall. Whether it's lusting for power that isn't ours to have, pursuing luxury where we should be generous, bulldozing another to make life easier for ourselves, turning a blind eye to the vulnerable, or even enjoying when we rise and another falls, we are all guilty in one way or another. We were all born into sin, which manifests itself in our lives in various ways.

And therein lies the scandal of the gospel—Jesus didn't die for innocent little Primroses. He died for the cruel rulers of the Capitol, for President Snow! Where Katniss sacrificed herself for the innocent, Jesus sacrificed Himself for the guilty, even for His enemies. How unexpected! A higher and different way indeed.

Where we would have tried to bring ourselves back to God in a million wrong ways—as passages like Psalm 22 and Isaiah 53 show us—Jesus came as a Suffering Servant to reconcile us to God through sacrifice—a most surprising solution. After all, it doesn't seem like blood would make a person clean. Nor does it seem logical that wounds would heal or that death would produce life. Yet this is the case with the gospel—God, in His higher and heavenly wisdom, made a plan to bring lost children back to Himself in a way that would turn all human expectations upside down. Instead of letting us be trampled for our treachery, Jesus came into our world, born as one of us, died on the cross, and took the trampling for us. There was simply no other way to reconcile us to God.

WHEN IT COMES TO HUMANITY'S SIN, NO ONE WANTS TO ENTER INTO THAT KIND OF DARKNESS AND WILLINGLY BEAR THE BRUTAL PUNISHMENT FOR IT. UNLESS, AGAIN, LOVE IS PART OF THE EQUATION. AND FOR JESUS, IT WAS.

There's only one person who can go into a world worse than the Capitol, pay its corruption and treachery in full, and come out victorious—and that unexpected victor is Jesus. This reality is what Advent is all about. Though He could have stayed right where He was, Jesus volunteered to come into the fray of humanity and sacrifice Himself so that all its wayward traitors could be brought back to God. The answer for separation was sacrifice. How astonishingly unexpected!

> Who in your life needs to hear the message of Advent—that Jesus came into the world to bring him or her back to God through Christ's sacrifice?

How thankful we should be that God's ways—His thoughts, His solutions, His wisdom, His perspective—are higher than ours! Sometimes, even though we know this truth, we have a hard time believing it in the everyday situations we face, don't we? Odd, isn't it, that we believe God's unexpected ways can be trusted with things as important as our salvation and eternity, but not with the details and daily burdens of our lives?

TAKE SOME TIME TO READ ISAIAH 53 (FOCUSING ON VERSE 7) AND MATTHEW 27 (FOCUSING ON VERSES 11-14).

> Regarding the Jewish expectation of a coming Messiah, what about Isaiah 53 strikes you as baffling or unexpected? How did Jesus fulfill these unexpected prophecies?

> Take a moment to pray and thank God that His thoughts and ways are so much higher than our own.

PRAYING WITH HOPE

by Mary Margaret West

First, read Hebrews 4:14-16.

When my dad was a kid, his family had a party telephone line with their neighbors, which meant several families shared a phone line. You could pick up the phone at your house and listen in on other people's conversations, but you couldn't start a phone call until they were done. My mom often talks about how, in her hometown, the operator had to connect you to whomever you were calling because you couldn't dial them directly. You told the operator the number, and she connected you.

Now, we're directly connected wherever we go. I used to love the feeling of being disconnected on a plane, but now it's easy to connect to Wi-Fi on most flights; we can stay in touch with our family and friends who are thirty thousand feet below us.

There are times I wish I wasn't so accessible, times I want to put all my electronic devices on airplane mode or turn them off for a while. Because most social apps have some sort of messaging feature, now I have to remember whether someone sent me a text, a direct message, an email, or actually called me on the phone. It's a lot to keep track of!

While being constantly connected can be overwhelming for us, it's never over-whelming to God. Because of Jesus, we have direct access to the Father. He never cuts us off, ignores our messages, or gets tired of hearing from us. In fact, He wants us to stay connected to Him all the time. God is more accessible and reliable than anyone else we know, but we often pull away from Him and gravi-tate toward things and people who will never meet the true need of our hearts.

Do you always feel as if God is accessible to you? Why or why not?

When Jesus was crucified and He breathed His final breath, the temple veil was torn in two from top to bottom, signifying that all people from that moment forward have direct access to God (Heb. 9:1-15). We don't have to sit in a confessional, find an intercessor, or make a blood sacrifice. We are able, at any moment, to have direct access to God because of Jesus Christ. Jesus is our Savior and our High Priest. We need Him in a desperate way that words can't describe, but we often forget our need for Him.

Many of us think we have to "fix ourselves" after we've sinned, and most certainly before we pray. But God wants us to come as we are—sins, scars, and all the baggage we so readily carry around. As Hebrews 4:14-16 reminds us, Jesus has already made the way clear.

The more you pray and talk to God, the more you'll realize that He's not a far-off, distant God, but One who is close and knows each of us intimately. Unlike a party phone line, we don't have to worry about anyone listening in on our conversations with God. It's just between us. This intimate relationship we have with the Father should give us great hope as we pray, because we know He hears us, loves us, and will do what's absolutely best for us.

> How does praying fuel your hope in God and in the outcomes He has planned for the situations you bring before Him?

Part of prayer is bringing our requests before God and waiting with anticipation on His answers, but in prayer we also realize how dependent we are on Him. A friend of mine often begins her prayers with, "God, I confess that I need You." This simple prayer reminds me that when I come to God, I'm in desperate need of Him. I need His help, wisdom, forgiveness, hope, peace, and so many of the other things He provides.

> When was the last time you confessed your need for God? Do you recognize that you need Him?

JESUS CAME SO THAT WE COULD HAVE FULL ACCESS TO THE FATHER. HE WANTS US TO APPROACH THE THRONE OF GRACE WITH OUR PRAYERS AND TO BE BOLD ABOUT IT.

Reread Hebrews 4:14-16. What does it look like for you to "approach the throne of grace with boldness"?

How does knowing Jesus faced difficulty on earth give you boldness to approach God in prayer?

Jesus is able "to sympathize with our weaknesses" (v. 15), meaning He knows the suffering and pain and temptation we endure because He endured it Himself, yet He was without sin. He was hurt. He was tempted. He was betrayed. He faced difficulty and opposition. He was ridiculed and mocked.

Jesus cried out to the Father in some of His darkest moments. And, because of His sacrifice, we can do the same. When we approach God with boldness, Scripture tells us we will "receive mercy and find grace to help us in time of need" (v. 16). God is faithful to meet us at our point of need; He never leaves us empty-handed. His grace and mercy are abundant and present, no matter what.

Before you close your study for today, approach the throne of grace with boldness and hope. Is there a need in your life you haven't yet asked God to meet? Is there healing you're desperate for God to bring? Who do you need to reconcile with, but it doesn't seem possible? What thing feels too small and insignificant to lay at His feet? Sister, be bold today. Ask God to move mountains. Trust that He is faithful to you, even when it feels like you're alone. Pray boldly, wait expectantly, and trust our sovereign God with how He answers those prayers.

NO MATTER WHERE YOU ARE OR WHO YOU ARE, YOU HAVE DIRECT ACCESS TO GOD BECAUSE OF JESUS. PRAISE GOD!

DAY 4

HOPE IN THE SILENCE

by Michelle R. Hicks

First, read Deuteronomy 31:6.

What is the longest period of time you've waited for an answer to prayer? How did you feel as you waited? Forgotten? Discouraged? Frustrated?

Are there any unanswered prayers in your life right now? Think back to what you journaled on p. 16. How do you remain hopeful in God's seeming silence?

We often grow restless and fearful when we feel like God is silent, when we're waiting on Him to act but He seems absent. How would you feel if you and your descendants didn't hear from God for four hundred years? If a specific prayer went unanswered that long?

The time between when the Old Testament ends and the New Testament begins is called the Intertestamental Period, a four hundred-year time span when God seemed silent. The people depended on prophets to hear from God, but between Malachi and John the Baptist, there was no prophet speaking to Israel.

ALL THE PEOPLE OF ISRAEL HEARD FOR FOUR HUNDRED YEARS WAS SILENCE.

By the end of the Old Testament, the Jewish people had returned to Israel from Babylonian captivity. The temple had been rebuilt, and the Law and the priesthood had been restored. However, spiritual apathy and indifference had set in. The Israelites oppressed others (Mal. 3:5), broke their marriage covenants (2:13-16), and stopped tithing (3:8). The priests didn't fear the Lord and failed to teach the people the ways of God (2:1-9). Yet, even though God's people were unfaithful to Him, He remained faithful to them.

READ DEUTERONOMY 31:6 AGAIN AND MALACHI 4:5-6.

What do you think God wanted His people to understand from these verses?

The promise Moses gave Joshua in Deuteronomy remained true even in the Intertestamental Period. During that time, the light of hope dimmed as the silence of God grew. It appeared God was absent, but He wasn't. He was with them during that four hundred-year period. And He was gracious to remind them that He wasn't going to forget them by closing the Old Testament with a promise—He was going to send a great spiritual reformer, a second Elijah, to rescue them.

After Malachi, there were many changes that took place. The Persians conquered the Babylonians, and then the Greeks conquered the Persians, led by Alexander the Great. The Hellenistic culture Alexander helped usher in emphasized education, individualism, and the Greek ideas of health, wealth, and competition.

The Jews were treated well throughout these various rules, but they experienced tremendous changes to their culture. During the Greek rule the Jewish people adopted the Greek language and many of the Greek customs. At the same time, eight groups rose up to resist the influence of the Greeks and to preserve the history, culture, and traditions of the Hebrew people. Three of these groups are familiar to us: the Pharisees, the Sadducees, and the Essenes.[6]

As they resisted the influence of Greek culture on a small scale, a turning point came when the temple was desecrated and a statue of Zeus was placed in the holy of holies. Enraged, a band of Jews rose up, led by the Maccabees, and drove the foreigners from their land.

The Maccabees cleansed the temple and rededicated it. When it came time to light the temple's menorah—"the gold candelabrum whose seven branches represented knowledge and creation and were meant to be kept burning every night"[7]—they searched the temple but only found one small jar of oil bearing the pure seal of the high priest. Miraculously, the small jar of oil burned for eight days until a new supply of oil could be brought to the temple. From then on the Jewish people celebrated the miracle of the oil by observing the eight-day Festival of Dedication (John 10:22-23,37-38), commonly known as Hanukkah.

Just as the Menorah stayed lit for those eight days during the four hundred years of silence, God had a plan, soon to be revealed, that would reignite the hope of the Jewish people.

READ GALATIANS 4:4-5.

What do these verses teach us?

What do you think the phrase at the beginning of verse 4 means: "when the time came to completion"?

According to these verses, why was Jesus born when He was born?

Although God seemed silent and distant during the Intertestamental Period, in reality, He never stopped working on behalf of His people. When the time had fully come, God revealed His plan. The light of hope that had grown dim for four hundred years would shine brightly as God demonstrated His gracious love in the most deliberate and intentional way—with the birth of the Rescuer.

During the times in our lives when God seems silent, He's often working in ways we can't see or understand to prepare us for what He has next. During the four hundred years before the birth of Jesus, a lot changed. Cultures merged. Both Jews and pagans were dissatisfied with religion. The Greeks, Romans, and other nations were questioning the validity of polytheism. The Scriptures were translated into other languages. Roads were built, and most people were free to travel. When Israel came under Roman rule around 63 BC, hope and faith were low for God's people. They were convinced the only thing that could save them and their faith was the appearance of the Messiah.

God, in His supreme wisdom, had the world primed for the Messiah. After years of not hearing from God, the Hebrew people were set up for the Word to come alive.

During the times when God seems silent and you feel forgotten, remind yourself of Deuteronomy 31:6:

> Be strong and courageous; don't be terrified or afraid of them. For the LORD your God is the one who will go with you; he will not leave you or abandon you.

God will never leave you. He is working out His plan, preparing the way for your next step, even when you can't see it.

As John Piper wrote,

> God is always doing 10,000 things in your life, and you may be aware of three of them.[8]

IN HIS TIME, GOD'S PLANS AND PURPOSES WILL BE ACCOMPLISHED.

As you reflect on all God was doing during the four hundred years when He seemed silent, think about your own seasons of waiting. Can you look back and see how God was working in ways hidden from you at the time? How can those experiences help you now as you wait?

Think of two people in your life who need a personal relationship with Jesus Christ. How might you share the truth of the gospel with them?

THE LIGHT OF HOPE

by Mickey Pitts

First, read Isaiah 9:2.

I grew up in Northeastern Oklahoma, smack-dab in the middle of what is commonly referred to as Tornado Alley. I have memories of being woken up in the night, grabbing my pillow, blanket, favorite stuffed animal, and a tiny flashlight, and hunkering down with our family poodle in our "safe room," otherwise known as the downstairs coat closet! For me, it wasn't the tornadoes that caused the most fear, but rather the darkness of the closet. The inability to see what was around me or what was ahead of me caused me great anxiety. The minutes seemed like hours as I waited for the light to come, but when it did, suddenly all my fear dissipated and I finally felt hope.

> Were you afraid of the dark as a child? If so, can you remember how being in the dark made you feel?

As we learned yesterday, the people of God weren't strangers to the darkness. After not hearing from God for four hundred years, the Israelites experienced a lot of confusion and uncertainty. They were in need of hope, and the words of the Old Testament prophet Isaiah, spoken hundreds of years earlier, could bring them just that. Isaiah had knowledge of a great Light who would be coming.

> The people walking in darkness have seen a great light;
> a light has dawned on those living in the land of darkness.
>
> *Isaiah 9:2*

Instead of focusing on the fear and anxiety of the darkness, Isaiah's prophecies were messages of hope for the coming of a Light, which we know to be Jesus.

Jesus said,

> I am the light of the world. Anyone who follows me will never walk in the darkness but will have the light of life.

John 8:12

Can you imagine it? After living in darkness for generations, God's people were promised eternal light and life.

Isaiah prophesied other names for this Light. In Isaiah 9:6b, the prophet said, "He will be named Wonderful Counselor, Mighty God, Eternal Father, Prince of Peace." Even these names themselves sound like hope! Everything God's people were longing for would be fulfilled in Jesus.

Let's take a few minutes to reflect on the names of Jesus in Isaiah 9:6b. Next to each name, write a description or an example of how Jesus filled that role during His time on earth.

NAME	DESCRIPTION
Wonderful Counselor	_____
Mighty God	_____
Eternal Father	_____
Prince of Peace	_____

Do any of these names for Jesus stand out to you in particular? If so, why?

In Matthew 1, we learn just how Jesus would enter the world. If you're like me, you have a tendency to want to skip long genealogical lists in the Bible; they seem tedious and unimportant. But the reality is they are very important! Matthew 1 isn't a list of random people's names, but rather confirmation that Jesus fulfilled all the Old Testament prophecies about the Messiah. Jesus came into the world exactly as prophesied. He is who He claimed to be!

Below are two names mentioned in the genealogy of Christ. Take a few minutes to read about these relatives of Jesus:

- Rahab (Josh. 2:1-21; 6:22-25; Matt. 1:5)

- David (2 Sam. 11:1-17; Matt. 1:6b)

Jesus' heritage wasn't made up of perfect people. After all, you just read that the bloodline of Christ includes a prostitute and a king who got a married woman pregnant and then had her husband killed! However, despite their sin and imperfections, God used them to bring the Light of life into the world.

I don't know about you, but reading about the imperfections in Jesus' lineage helps me understand that I don't have to be perfect to be used by God. All the people listed in Matthew 1 were used because they had a role to play in bringing the only perfect One to us, not because they were perfect themselves.

Just as God used ordinary, imperfect people to bring Jesus into the world, He can use ordinary, imperfect people like us to bring the hope of Jesus to others.

> In the space below, write a prayer to God, asking Him to help you bring the hope of Jesus to others.

> If you're a follower of Jesus, how might you be a bearer of hope for others today? What are some practical ways you can help those living in darkness to find light in Jesus?

If you haven't yet made the decision to follow Jesus, the good news is the Light of life is available to you today (see p. 143). Jesus is still—and will always be—our "Wonderful Counselor, Mighty God, Eternal Father, Prince of Peace" (Isa. 9:6b). We don't have to sit in the darkness of our coat closet, waiting out the storm anymore. The Light of life has come. He is who He claimed to be, and He came to bring light and hope to a weary world. Will you follow Him?

HOW ARE YOU A BEARER OF HOPE FOR PEOPLE? HOW ARE YOU ADVANCING THE HOPE OF JESUS?

MAKE A CHRISTMAS
SPICE WREATH

by Larissa Arnault Roach

Set the tone for the Christmas season by creating a lovely aromatic wreath (or garland or ornaments) you can enjoy all month long. Usher in holiday scents by using dried oranges, bay leaves, and cinnamon sticks. Do this activity on your own or make it a festive craft night with friends or family! If you have enough supplies, encourage everyone to make two—one to keep and one to deliver to a neighbor who might need a little Christmas cheer.

GATHER*

- 3 Oranges
- 2 Apples
- Large embroidery needle
- Twine or floral wire
- Cinnamon sticks
- Whole bay leaves

You may need to adjust the amount of supplies depending on the size of the wreath you choose to make.

DIRECTIONS

Prepare the oranges and apples a day ahead. Preheat the oven to 200°F. Slice fruit ¼-inch thick with a serrated knife and arrange them in a single layer on a wire rack on a baking sheet. Or, place the slices directly on the oven rack. (If using this method, place a baking sheet on the lower rack to catch any that fall.) Bake for 4 hours, turning a few times. Allow slices to sit overnight to continue the drying process.

Assemble the wreath or garland. If using twine, start by threading a large needle. Tightly wrap the twine or wire around a cinnamon stick (or drill holes in cinnamon sticks to string them) and then add an orange slice and an apple slice, several bay leaves, and another orange slice. Repeat until you reach the end of the twine or wire. Tie up the ends, hang, and enjoy!

As you breathe in the wintry scents of orange, bay leaves, and cinnamon, consider Mary's anticipation of Christ taking His first breath. Meditate on the hope Jesus embodies for all people—friends, family, enemies, coworkers, strangers—even as a helpless Babe.

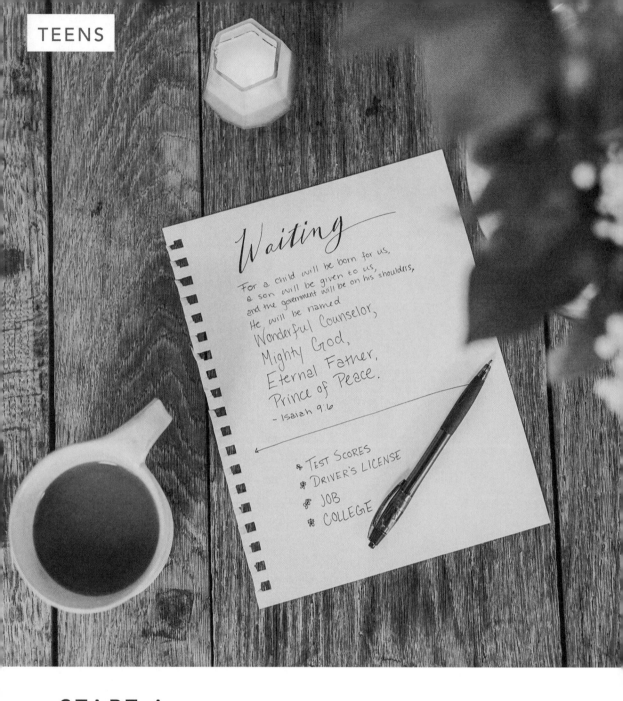

Waiting

For a child will be born for us,
a son will be given to us,
and the government will be on his shoulders,
He will be named
Wonderful Counselor,
Mighty God,
Eternal Father,
Prince of Peace.
— Isaiah 9:6

✤ TEST SCORES
✤ DRIVER'S LICENSE
✤ JOB
✤ COLLEGE

START A
LIST ABOUT WAITING

by Karen Daniel

Waiting can feel like one of the most difficult things we do. Sometimes it's tempting to think nothing will ever change. But God is never still or silent. Throughout the Old Testament, God promised to send a Savior to rescue His people. Between the periods of the Old Testament and the New Testament, however, the Israelites didn't hear from God for four hundred years. Had He forgotten them? Or was their waiting intentional?

Despite the best arguments for calling this the "instant gratification generation," your teenager knows very well what it means to wait. When they were little, how many times did you tell them to "wait for Mommy to finish what she's doing," or "wait until I put in this last load of laundry," or even "we can get that for you next Christmas, but not this one."

Before long, our little ones are anxiously waiting for the day they will become teenagers, get their driver's license, and perhaps even a car. They wait to hear back on job applications, test scores, and responses from universities. They spend most of their high school years counting down the days until they get to be seniors, and after that counting down to graduation. To them, their entire lives have seemed like one long season of waiting.

Take some time this week to talk with your teen about what it is he's currently waiting for, those events or answers that seem like they'll never come. Start a list and place it where you'll both see it regularly, like on the fridge or on his bathroom mirror. Add this verse to the top:

> For a child will be born
> for us, a son will be given
> to us, and the government
> will be on his shoulders.
> He will be named Wonderful
> Counselor, Mighty God,
> Eternal Father, Prince
> of Peace.
>
> *Isaiah 9:6*

Pray together about the things your teen listed and the hope this verse offers. Point out that God always keeps His promises. Remind him that while the Israelites waited centuries for the promised Messiah, we live in the reality of that promise. We have a living Savior we can go to every day if we've invited Christ into our hearts. We don't have to wait to go to Him.

MAKE A
PAPER CHAIN

by Bekah Stoneking

God created everything—including you and me—and everything God created was good and perfect.

Until something terrible happened.

When the first people chose to follow their way instead of God's way, sin entered the world. Everything was broken. People were separated from God. And since then, the whole world has become desperate for a Rescuer to come and make all things new.

Everyone is waiting and wanting. The things that hurt you or make you wish for something better may be different than the things your friends or parents or neighbors long for, but we're all hoping and waiting together. As you wait and pray, trust that God is good, He has a plan, and He always keeps His promises.

During Christmas we celebrate and remember that God kept His promise to send Jesus to earth to rescue us. Because of the Christmas promise, we can have hope that Jesus will return for us. God has not left us hopeless. He sent Jesus, and He has promised that Jesus will come again and make everything new. The anticipation you have waiting for Christmas day should remind you of the anticipation you have waiting for Jesus' return.

DIRECTIONS

To help you count down the days until Christmas, make a paper chain. Cut strips of colorful construction paper (or any kind of fun paper)—one for each day until December 25th. Work with your family to write encouraging words, Bible verses, and evidences of God's grace on each strip. Tape or staple the strips together to make a chain. Every day, remove one link and read what's written on it. Remember God's faithfulness and talk about the hope you have in Him. Pray and thank God for sending Jesus to be our Savior.

PEACE

WEEK 2

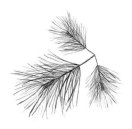

YONDER BREAKS A NEW AND GLORIOUS MORN

by Elizabeth Hyndman

When I think of Advent, I often think of the familiar idiom, "It's always darkest before the dawn."

In our history as the people of God, we see darkness turn into light in Advent. In the years between the end of the Book of Malachi and Matthew 1, things got dark. Persecution, confusion, and wondering plagued the people of God. What about His promise? What about the Messiah?

Today, we face a similar darkness. No one needs to be convinced of our need for peace. Wars, natural disasters, political unrest, violence, prejudice, famine, and disease plague us, just to name a few headlines. Each of us has inner battles as well. We're fighting chaos of a different kind internally—sins, temptations, fears. The world can seem very dark.

But "yonder breaks a new and glorious morn," to quote the carol.[1] Morning comes. Peace has come.

When the world seemed too dark, too scary, too chaotic, the Prince of Peace came to earth. The angel declared,

> Don't be afraid, for look,
> I proclaim to you good
> news of great joy that will
> be for all the people.

Luke 2:10

And then a multitude joined in declaring,

> Glory to God in the
> highest heaven, and peace
> on earth to people he
> favors!

Luke 2:14

Don't be afraid! I have good news—good news for all people. All those living in darkness and chaos. All those praying for peace in the darkest of days. All those afraid but hopeful. Here is the morning! Here is the Light! Here is the Peace!

Living on this side of that "new and glorious morn," we aren't completely free from the darkness. We await the final morning when we will no longer "need the sun or the moon to shine on it, because the glory of God illuminates it, and its lamp is the Lamb" (Rev. 21:23).

While we wait for the second Advent, we wait with hope and with peace.

This week, as we study, we'll see what it means that Peace came to earth in the form of the long-awaited Messiah. We'll look for ways we can advance the peace of Christ in a world all too familiar with the darkness. And we'll celebrate the new and glorious morning!

What from last week's personal study was particularly impactful for you?

What do you think of when you hear the word *peace*? A lack of conflict, chaos, and confusion? A feeling of serenity or stillness?

We live in a world fraught with tragedy. Do you think it's even possible to have peace in this day and age, when things seem so out of control?

In 2 Thessalonians 3:16, Paul wrote, "Now may the Lord of peace himself give you peace at all times and in every way" (NIV). Does knowing peace is available to you at all times change your view of what peace is?

As you close in prayer, ask God for a fresh perspective of His gift of peace. Pray for those in a particularly turbulent time, for God to grant them His peace that passes all understanding.

_____

_____

_____

_____

_____

_____

_____

_____

_____

_____

PEACE WITH GOD

by Mary C. Wiley

First, read Romans 3:23 and Ephesians 2:13.

Take a moment to finish these sentences:

"World _____" —The quintessential beauty queen answer to what they want most.

"If I could only get some _____ and quiet." —A busy toddler mom

"I just don't have _____ about it." —That guy in those awkward middle school years who used this as an excuse to break up with you or your best friend

Peace seems to be what everyone is seeking but few find. Often, we think of peace as a ceasing from striving, a stillness, or quiet. But true peace—the kind that will be sustained for all of eternity—is far better than even the best stillness in a chaotic season.

In the beginning there was peace. Peace wasn't equated with stillness but with nearness to God. God walked with His people in the garden in the cool of the day, and all was just as it was meant to be.

Yet, as we read earlier in Genesis 3, peace with God and unrestricted access to His presence were interrupted when Adam and Eve sinned and were sent away from the garden of Eden. Today, we're in the same situation they once were. We, too, are separated from God because of sin, lacking peace with Him.

READ ROMANS 3:23.

What does this verse say about our condition?

God has very clear standards. His holiness demands perfection, which is why Adam and Eve's sin had such harsh consequences and why our sin is enough to separate us from God. The Greek word translated as "have sinned" in Romans 3:23 is often used to describe an archer who misses the target—"to miss the mark."[2] God revealed to us His perfect standard of living, and we missed the mark.

Missing God's mark of perfect living isn't just a disappointment. Romans 6:23 says the wages, or rightful payment, for our sin "is death." Sin separates us from God and requires punishment. Yet God, in His mercy, made a way for His people to be in His presence and experience peace with Him.

Before Jesus came to the earth, God met with His people through a high priest in the tabernacle and later the temple. Sin was confessed and sacrifices were made. God sought to give His people peace with Him as they trusted Him to keep His promise to send a Messiah. This Messiah would make all things right again and restore peace throughout the earth.

READ ROMANS 3:21-28.

What characteristics of God do we see in this passage?

Write verse 22 below. Underline what this verse says about how we have peace with God.

Most original readers of Paul's Letter to the Romans were familiar with the sacrificial system and its place in Israel's history. The temple was a place of worship but also a place that smelled like the burning flesh of animals. To atone for one's sin, a spotless animal had to be brought to the priest, and the person's sin was symbolically placed on it. The animal took on sin's required penalty—death—as a substitute.

Similarly, Jesus, the spotless Lamb of God, took on the wrath we deserve. Our sin was laid upon Him, and in exchange, He clothed us in His righteousness. In addition to giving us His righteousness, Jesus has also given us His Sonship. We aren't just forgiven; we are restored to nearness with God as a parent and a child.

BECAUSE OF JESUS, WE CAN HAVE PEACE WITH GOD AND ACCESS TO HIS PRESENCE.

READ EPHESIANS 2:13.

What does this passage say has been done as a result of the blood of Jesus?

Ultimate peace is being near to the One we once considered an enemy. Romans 8:7 says we were "hostile to God" before we trusted in Jesus. Yet, through Jesus' payment for our sin on the cross, all who trust Him have peace with God. This peace isn't a temporary feeling brought about by good, stress-free situations. Instead, eternal peace flows from a heart that has been made new.

Leviticus 7:11-21 gives us the framework for how to respond to the joy of knowing we have peace with God.

READ LEVITICUS 7:11-21.

In the Old Testament, God's people made peace offerings (also known as fellowship offerings). A peace offering wasn't a required sacrifice; it was a voluntary expression of gratitude for God's intervention and deliverance. Unlike a sin offering, a peace offering wasn't completely consumed by fire. Instead, the person offering the sacrifice, along with his family and friends, shared a meal and ate the meat together.[3] God basically told His followers to throw a party because of the joy of being restored to right relationship with Him!

We don't offer a sacrifice in a temple today, but joy and gratitude can still be our goal.

What's the difference between having peace with God and feeling peaceful? Are they always present together? Explain.

If you're in Christ, you have peace with God. This peace doesn't change with feelings, and it isn't temporary. God is peace, and He is unchanging and unmoving. God has come near. His presence is our peace.

God is peace, and in Him is no unrest, chaos, or confusion. He is worthy to be worshiped for His gift of making us right with Him through Jesus. Choose a way to celebrate His gift of peace today—maybe you can spend some time thanking Him in prayer, talking about it around the dinner table, or sharing a meal with friends.

Hallelujah! We have peace with God.

DAY 2

PEACE IN GOD

by Jessica Yentzer

First, read Luke 2:13–14.

One of my favorite moments of the Christmas season is the final song of the Christmas Eve service at my church. The overhead lights are turned out and we're left with just the Advent candles burning at the front of the sanctuary. One person lights his small disposable candle using the center Advent candle—the Christ candle—and then he lights his neighbor's candle, and the congregation slowly passes the flame around the room until everyones' candles are lit. As the flame is passed around, someone starts singing "Silent Night, Holy Night" and the song spreads through the crowd, much like the flame.

As a child, I loved getting my very own candle; it was a fun way to celebrate Christ's birth. As an adult, I've noticed myself letting out a sweet sigh as I savor the wonder of Christ's coming while the *a cappella* carol fills the room. Sometimes I feel like the busyness and stress of the holidays cause me to hold my breath—until this final song. As I exhale and sing "Sleep in heavenly peace"[4] I feel just that—peace.

The feeling of holding your breath through life—of waiting for the hard things to pass—is something most of us are familiar with. We've probably all walked through hard things—some tragic and some disappointing—and it can be difficult to know how to find peace in the midst of the pain.

> Have you found yourself holding your breath or pushing through hard seasons without peace? How would your circumstances or day-to-day living look different if you were experiencing the peace of God?

God promised peace to His people throughout the pages of Scripture, so it's important for us to return to God's Word and remind ourselves of this promise.

If we visit the familiar story of Christ's birth, we see a promise of peace from the angels who visited the shepherds:

> Suddenly there was a multitude of the heavenly host with the angel, praising God and saying: Glory to God in the highest heaven, and peace on earth to people he favors!
>
> *Luke 2:13-14*

This heavenly praise immediately followed the angel of the Lord's news that Christ was born. It seems significant that one of the few words the heavens rang out with was *peace*. Peace was a big part of Christ's coming—the Prince of Peace came to the earth to bring us peace.

Paul described how Christ's coming brings us peace. Read Romans 5:1 and write it below.

In other words, because Christ came to earth and died and rose again, we are declared righteous in God's sight when we place our faith in Jesus. How freeing this truth is for us! No matter what trials or circumstances we walk through, we can have peace because we know we belong to God.

How does the truth of Romans 5:1 bring you peace, even in hard circumstances? What freedom do you find in remembering you have been declared righteous through Jesus?

It can be tempting for me to see others experiencing God's peace and believe the lie that the promise of peace is for everyone but me. When I'm overcome with worry about a situation, it can feel like peace is a far-off dream, something that just isn't possible for me. But if we look back at Luke 2:14, we see the angels offer peace to the "people [God] favors." And Romans 5 helps us interpret whom the angels were talking about. If we have placed our faith in Christ and

His sacrifice, we have been declared righteous and are among those whom God favors. The promise of peace is for us!

> Have you been tempted to believe the lie that the promise of peace is for others but not for you? How do Luke 2:14 and Romans 5:1 encourage you that God offers *you* peace?

When I doubt God's promise of peace, I know it's because I'm trying to walk through a situation in my own strength. And, if I'm honest, the "peace" I often seek is a solution to my difficult circumstances, not a quiet heart in the midst of the storm. But God's peace is more about the promise of His ultimate victory through Christ. It's so much bigger than my circumstances. I can have peace in the waiting, knowing that God already has the victory.

> I have told you these things so that in me you may have peace. You will have suffering in this world. Be courageous! I have conquered the world.
>
> *John 16:33*

Christ has the ultimate victory over death and over all the things that worry us. He is in control, and He is working for our good (Rom. 8:28).

> How does Christ's victory give you hope and peace in your current circumstances? How does His promise in John 16:33 transform your perspective of suffering?

What does it look like for us to embrace the promise of peace in God? It means being totally dependent on God to provide for us and walk through life's hard things with us. The short version? It means trusting Him fully.

You will keep the mind that is dependent on you in perfect peace, for it is trusting in you.

Isaiah 26:3

I've found that the process of surrender is a constant for me. Paul encouraged us to "pray constantly" (1 Thess. 5:17); in the same way, we have to continually turn our eyes toward God and keep our minds dependent on Him. I can't do this on my own; I need the Lord to sustain and provide for me. When I stop relying on myself and trust in the Lord to walk with me, there is freedom and, in turn, peace.

READ PHILIPPIANS 4:6-7.

How does prayer give you peace?

How can you more fully step into what Paul challenged us to do in Philippians 4?

There is nothing too big or small to place at the Lord's feet when we approach the throne of grace in prayer. He can handle our burdens, our frustrations, and our hardships. He can handle the messiness.

This season, bring your worries to the Lord in prayer. Ask Him to help you trust Him more fully with the things that weigh on you. Ask Him to help you experience the peace He promises in His Word.

MAY YOU WALK IN GOD'S PEACE IN THE EVERYDAY MOMENTS OF LIFE AND IN THE HARDEST SEASONS OF LIFE, BOTH DURING ADVENT AND ALL YEAR LONG.

PEACE ON EARTH

by Rachel Shaver

First, read Luke 1:5–38 and Matthew 1:18–25.

If you were stuck in a field full of quicksand, what would you do? Would you panic? Or would you remain calm? I know what I'd do: Panic, party of one. But contrary to human instinct, they say the best way to escape what can only be described as certain death is to remain calm, call out for help, and await a rescue.

The promise of rescue was what God's people held onto generation after generation. In Genesis 3:15, God told Satan, "I will put hostility between you and the woman, and between your offspring and her offspring. He will strike your head, and you will strike his heel." In other words, "A child of Eve (Jesus) will crush you one day, Satan; I will defeat you and rescue My people."

God's people suffered hardship. Deep down, they knew they needed to be rescued and believed God would send a Messiah to restore peace, but they had a tendency to forget. So God gave His people prophets and judges to remind them of His promise. And then, as we discovered last week, there was a period in which God seemed silent—a period of four hundred years to be exact.

But in the Gospel of Matthew, God broke His silence and kept His promise of a Rescuer. And He didn't do it with parades, trumpets, or clanging symbols. He did it with His angel, Gabriel, who appeared to Zechariah, His humble servant.

READ LUKE 1:5-25.

Zechariah was a married, childless priest, who, as Scripture very politely says, was "well along in years" (v. 7). He was chosen to enter the sanctuary of the Lord to pray and burn incense. (This, by the way, wasn't something all priests were able to do. There were thousands of priests in Israel at the time, so to enter the sanctuary and participate in this activity was a once-in-a-lifetime experience.) We can speculate about Zechariah's prayers—some say they were for a child, some say they were for the salvation of God's people, and others say they could have been for the coming Messiah.[5] Little did he know, all of these prayers were about to be answered.

An angel named Gabriel appeared to Zechariah. What did Gabriel immediately tell Zechariah (see vv. 11-12)?

Gabriel was no wimpy angel. He stood in the presence of God, so he was probably pretty sturdy. (He also appeared to Daniel, who fell on his face at the sight of him, indicating that Gabriel's appearance was likely quite frightening. See Dan. 8:17.)

That being said, what did Gabriel tell Zechariah was going to happen?

That's right, my friends. Zechariah and his equally "well along in years" wife, Elizabeth, were going to have a baby named John. We know him as John the Baptist—the one Jesus called the greatest among men (Matt. 11:11). Zechariah's life got flipped upside down by a warrior angel who appeared to him in a quiet sanctuary. His decades-long plea for a child was being answered despite life circumstances that said it was impossible. When Gabriel spoke his first words, "Do not be afraid" (Luke 1:13), to Zechariah that day, God broke His silence with news that He was paving a way for all of His people to have peace on earth and peace with Him: "Your son, Zechariah? He's going to point people to the great rescue that God has been promising to your Fathers. The One you've been praying for? He's coming."

READ LUKE 1:26-38.

This time, Gabriel appeared to Mary, the mother of Jesus. We can't be certain of her exact age, but she was likely fairly young—between twelve and fourteen, as that was the average age to be betrothed according to Jewish custom at that time. We also aren't sure what Mary was doing when Gabriel appeared to her, but I'm going to go out on a limb here and say this angelic visitation came as a shock to her.

What did Gabriel tell Mary in verse 30?

There's our reminder again. "Do not be afraid, because, well, you're staring at an angel, and what I am about to say is a lot to take in." (I'm paraphrasing, of course.)

What did Gabriel tell Mary in verses 31-33?

"Hi, Mary. Look, I know you're engaged and a virgin, but you're going to be pregnant and birth the Savior and King of the world." (My paraphrase again.)

Mary obviously had some questions, but Gabriel reassured her. What did he say in verse 37? Write it below.

Again, there is so much we could unpack here, but we'd be camping out for days. Let's not miss this, though: More than the seeming impossibility of these circumstances and the inadequacy Mary likely felt as the one chosen for this task, Gabriel told Mary in so many words, "The Prince of Peace, the Son of God, the Messiah, the One you and generations before you have waited for? He's coming, Mary. The Rescuer is finally here."

READ MATTHEW 1:18-25.

Joseph and Mary weren't married yet, but she was pregnant. That presented a problem because Joseph and Mary hadn't "been together" yet. (It's all there in the Bible, folks.) Scripture tells us that Joseph was righteous and didn't want to publicly disgrace Mary, so he decided instead to divorce her in secret.

Not so fast, Joseph. As Joseph was sleeping one night, an angel appeared to him in a dream. Read verse 20. What did the angel tell Joseph?

You got it. "Don't be afraid, Joseph. This all seems a little crazy, but Mary is actually pregnant by the Holy Spirit. She's going to give birth to a Son. Name Him Jesus, because He is going to save people from their sins."

Did you catch that last part? *He is going to save people from their sins.*

Reread verse 23. What does *Immanuel* mean?

All of these angelic messages boil down to this: The great Rescuer, the One who will save people from their sins? He is now with us. The silence is broken! Peace has arrived!

Praise the Lord!

Think about the time you first heard the good news of Jesus. Who told you? Where were you?

What stops you from sharing Jesus with others? What makes you hesitate when God asks you to do something for Him?

Honestly, for me, it's fear—fear of what people will think or of how the interaction might infringe upon my comfort. It's interesting to me, though, that each time an angel delivered news to one of God's people, the angel immediately prefaced his message with, "Don't be afraid." Don't be afraid because you're now staring at an angel, but also, don't be afraid because of this thing God is telling you to do. It feels impossible, yes, but with God, nothing is impossible. And what He's asking you to do? It's amazing! He's choosing to use you to build His kingdom and bring Him glory. It's a privilege. Don't be afraid.

How can we break our silence and share the news about our great Rescuer with those who don't know Him?

Today, close in prayer. Thank God for sending His Son, the great Rescuer, and for the people who broke their silence and shared Jesus with you. Ask Him to help you break your silence and tell the world His good news.

IMMANUEL, FRIENDS. IMMANUEL—GOD WITH US.

PEACE, GOD'S GIFT TO YOU

by Betsy Langmade

First, read Isaiah 9:6; John 14:27; and 2 Thessalonians 3:16.

Among the prophetic names of Jesus in Isaiah 9:6 is one of my very favorites—the Prince of Peace. So often in my day-to-day life I feel an absence of peace. It only takes seeing a snippet of the news, or hearing of a friend's diagnosis, or a sideways conversation with my husband, and boom! My mind and heart are in a state of conflict and chaos. I suspect that happens to you too. But Isaiah 9:6 tells us Jesus is our Prince of Peace.

Gift giving in our home is a serious undertaking. We don't do anything extravagant, but the goal is for each person to know he or she was thought about—likes, hobbies, personality, needs—and know the special item was carefully selected. My hope is that every member of my family will feel valued for who they are as individuals. It makes me think of how our God sees us in the same way. His heart and gaze watch over us constantly, fully knowing our every doubt, weakness, joy, and sorrow. Because God loves us and knows us so intimately, He chose to give us a gift, one especially suited to meet our needs and bring us incomprehensible joy. It's a gift that has the potential to reign in our hearts no matter what circumstances are swirling around us.

In John's Gospel, Jesus was preparing His disciples for His imminent departure. It was not unlike the preparation of those we love as they get ready to pass from life to death. Usually our loved ones are intent on making certain they say all the important things before they pass on, and Jesus did the same. In John 13:34–14:26, Jesus told His beloved followers of a new command, of the way to the Father, of His oneness with the Father, of the coming Counselor (the Holy Spirit), and of His relationship to the Father. He was making sure they knew the most important things about Him and how to carry on once He was no longer physically with them.

Then Jesus gave them a tremendously important departing gift.

What gift did Jesus promise His disciples?

Jesus has given us *His* peace. "My peace I give to you." It's miraculous and mysterious but I believe He desired it to be oh-so practical too. His peace is not something we have to hope for or try to attain. It's His gift to us and the fruit of His Spirit living inside of us. When we trust Jesus for the forgiveness of our sins and receive the Holy Spirit, one of the manifestations of the Spirit in us is peace (Gal. 5:22-23).

Jesus went on to say, "I do not give to you as the world gives" (John 14:27). I think of all the things the world tries to pass off as peace—substances, do-it-yourself remedies, buckets of material possessions, fleeting pleasures, and empty promises. But these things are cheap substitutes for the real thing, for the lasting and enduring peace that passes understanding. I also think about the world's way of giving. They give with the expectation of getting something in return, something shiny but empty. But Jesus' gift of peace is pure and unconditional.

> In the very last sentence of verse 27 Jesus give us the most practical and precious part of His gift of peace. Write it below.

Do you see the invitation for us here to use our will? We need to act on His command.

Jesus first made it clear what He has provided for us—His peace. Then, He made it clear that because He has given us His peace, we don't need to *let* our hearts be full of fear and confusion and chaos. We can choose to hold onto His peace no matter what.

LET'S REMEMBER THAT THE ACT OF OUR WILL IS SUBMISSION TO THE SPIRIT. WE CAN NEVER FIX SELF WITH MORE SELF. WE'RE TRANSFORMED WHEN WE SUBMIT TO OUR COUNSELOR.

READ GALATIANS 5:22-23a.

Turn these verses into a prayer, inviting the Holy Spirit to reign in your heart. Write your prayer below.

In what ways are you experiencing the absence of God's gift of peace today?

Talk to God about your anxieties and fears right now, openly and honestly. Remember that His desire for you is to live in His peace. Despite your troubles, don't let your heart be overwhelmed. Will you live moment by moment today focusing on the peace that's yours by the power of the Holy Spirit?

Read 2 Thessalonians 3:16. How is this verse similar to John 14:27?

Do you have chaos, confusion, and conundrums swirling around you today? Is money tight? Are relationships fractured? Is the loss you feel overwhelming? I invite you to open your heart, posture your spirit, and receive the beautiful gift of peace from the Prince of Peace Himself—Jesus. He is waiting for you to fix your gaze on His perfection, His salvation, His faithfulness, and His peace.

Will you go back to John 14:27 now? Read it. And reread it. Read it out loud. Read it again like you mean to receive it. Write it out. Post it where you'll see it for the remainder of the Advent season. As His peace floods in, let your fear and anxiety be swept up in His great love. Let the gift of His peace reign in your mind and heart.

BECOMING A PEACEMAKER

by Connia Nelson

First, read Ephesians 2:14.

Have you ever been in a meeting or at an event when a controversial discussion turned from a healthy, spirited debate to an explosive, disruptive conversation? When that happens I often find myself looking for the nearest exit. But then a calming voice speaks in the midst of the disruption, diffusing heated words. That one person is somehow able to restore a sense of reasonableness back to the group. That person is a peacemaker.

When Jesus came to the earth, He brought peace to our chaotic world—He gave us peace with God and peace with others through God. And when He returns to fully and wholly redeem our world, we'll experience ultimate peace. I love how Isaiah described the eternal reign of the Prince of Peace:

> The wolf will dwell with the lamb,
> and the leopard will lie down with the goat.
> The calf, the young lion, and the fattened calf will be together,
> and a child will lead them.
> The cow and the bear will graze,
> their young ones will lie down together,
> and the lion will eat straw like cattle.
> An infant will play beside the cobra's pit,
> and a toddler will put his hand into a snake's den.
> They will not harm or destroy each other ...

Isaiah 11:6-9a

The ultimate Peacemaker will cover the earth and everything in it with peace.

READ EPHESIANS 2:11-18.

The Ephesians, the original readers of Paul's Letter, were largely non-Jewish (Gentile) Christians. In the ancient world, the designations of "the uncircumcised" and "the circumcised" (v. 11) meant more than just something physical; they described the difference between the non-elect and the elect covenant people of God. The Jewish people—the circumcised—considered the Gentiles—the uncircumcised—to be inferior. And the Gentiles weren't crazy about the Jews either.[6]

How does verse 12 describe the state of the Gentiles?

Verse 12 is a picture of our reality before Christ—we were completely hopeless. The point Paul was trying to make was that the distinction between the circumcised and the uncircumcised didn't matter, since circumcision is "done in the flesh by human hands" (v. 11). Both Jews and Gentiles, apart from Christ, are in the flesh and at war with Him and each other.

Look at verse 14. What does it say that Jesus is?

Jesus doesn't just give peace; He *is* peace. It's because He shed His blood on the cross that we can be at peace with God (Rom. 5:1). I am completely in awe of how Christ sacrificed Himself so that we could be reconciled to God and have peace with Him.

What's interesting is that, according to Ephesians 2, peace isn't the absence of conflict or hostility. Christ had to destroy hostility in order for peace to be established (v. 14). Even in the Old Testament, David asked about the peace (*shalom*) of his war (2 Sam. 11:7). Peace in the biblical context "covers wholeness, physical well-being, prosperity, security, good relations, and integrity."[7]

Being a peacemaker doesn't mean being a doormat and steering clear of conflict. Rather, a peacemaker "is someone who is actively seeking to reconcile people to God and to one another."[8] Peacemakers show grace and look for goodness. When they walk into a room they bring with them a sense of calmness, love, mercy, wisdom and patience. They exude the fruit of the Spirit (Gal. 5:22-23). Peacemakers glorify God and exemplify His character. They mediate disputes, improve understanding, and seek reconciliation. Peacemakers bring unity:

> Let the peace of Christ rule in your hearts, since as members of one body you were called to peace. And be thankful.
>
> *Colossians 3:15, NIV*

In what circumstances or relationship in your life can you be a peacemaker? Does knowing peace isn't the absence of conflict change the way you'll approach these situations?

When I think of how God created us all so differently, I marvel at His handiwork. We are products of our environment with vastly diverse experiences. As a result, we often disagree with each other, and it's OK to do that respectfully. But as believers, we should not let differences of opinion fracture our relationships. Paul wrote, "If possible, as far as it depends on you, live at peace with everyone" (Rom. 12:18). We have a responsibility to have peaceful relationships with everyone … "if possible" and "as far as it depends on" us. Unfortunately, that means peace isn't always possible. Even though we can choose to live at peace with someone, if that person doesn't choose the same, unity in that relationship isn't possible.

Write down any broken or damaged relationships in your life that need healing and restoration.

How can you honor God in reconciling the existing conflict?

Could peace in these relationships depend on you? How so?

When Jesus removed the barriers of hostility and hatred, He created a way for people to come together, restoring peace to hostile and damaged relationships and to the world. We all long for peace in our lives. But we can only have peace and come together as one if we have God in us, working through us. It is God in us that brings about peace.

Isn't it amazing how through one sacrifice of one Savior, we become a new creation in one Father? No longer are we separated from God, but one group of believers at peace with Him and with each other. As children of God we can exemplify His character by spreading both love and peace.

> Deceit is in the hearts of those who plot evil,
> but those who promote peace have joy.
>
> *Proverbs 12:20*

HOW CAN YOU BE A PEACEMAKER IN YOUR WORLD TODAY?

MAKE HOMEMADE
MARSHMALLOWS

by Larissa Arnault Roach

With the busyness of the Christmas season, it can be hard to find time to simply sit, reflect, and enjoy the beauty around you. Take this time to reflect on the peace of Christ that lives in you.

Stay up later than usual one evening (or get up while it's still dark), and turn off your phone and the TV. Using only the light from your Christmas tree and a few candles, sip mulled cider or hot cocoa as you pray for God to make you a bearer of peace during the most wonderful—but most hectic—time of the year.

Consider whipping up some homemade marshmallows to enjoy with your hot cocoa as you sip and savor the sights and smells of Christmas. Note: This recipe requires sitting overnight, so make them a day ahead!

GATHER (MAKES 20–40 MARSHMALLOWS)

- 3 packages unflavored gelatin
- 1 cup cold water, divided
- 1½ cups granulated sugar
- 1 cup light corn syrup
- ¼ teaspoon kosher salt
- 1 tablespoon pure vanilla extract
- ½ cup confectioners' sugar, plus more for dusting

DIRECTIONS

Combine the gelatin and ½ cup of cold water in the bowl of an electric mixer fitted with the whisk attachment, and allow to sit while you make the syrup.

Combine the sugar, corn syrup, salt, and ½ cup water in a small saucepan and cook over medium heat until the sugar dissolves. Raise the heat to high and cook until the syrup reaches 240°F on a candy thermometer, approximately 7 minutes. Remove from the heat.

With the mixer on low speed, slowly pour the sugar syrup into the dissolved gelatin. Put the mixer on high speed and whip until the mixture is very thick, about 15 minutes. Add the vanilla and mix thoroughly.

With a sieve (sifter), generously dust an 8"x12" nonmetal baking dish with confectioners' sugar. Pour the marshmallow mixture into the pan, smoothing the top with a lightly oiled spatula. Dust with more confectioners' sugar. Allow to stand uncovered overnight until it dries out. Turn the marshmallows onto a board and cut them into squares. Dust them with more confectioners' sugar if desired. Store in an airtight container for up to 3 weeks.

Recipe adapted from FoodNetwork.com.

SET ASIDE

TIME TO REST

by Karen Daniel

"Suddenly there was a multitude of the heavenly host with the angel, praising God and saying: Glory to God in the highest heaven, and peace on earth to people he favors!" (Luke 2:13-14).

As the semester begins to wind down and Christmas break approaches, remember that your teen wants to rest and celebrate the season as much as you want her to. But with practices and games filling up her calendar and the pressure of final exams and project deadlines looming, how can she possibly think about enjoying even a few moments of peace?

According to a 2019 Pew Research report, anxiety among teens is on the rise. Why are they so stressed out? Academics tops the list with 61 percent of teens saying they "feel a lot of pressure to get good grades."[9] Following is the pressure "to look good" (29 percent), "fit in socially" (28 percent), "be involved in extracurricular activities" (21 percent), and "be good at sports" (21 percent).[10]

Help your teen identify the pressures she's facing at school and in other areas of her life right now. Encourage her to start journaling her concerns and taking each one to God. And together, commit to memorizing the following passage from Philippians this week:

> Rejoice in the Lord always. I will say it again: Rejoice! Let your graciousness be known to everyone. The Lord is near. Don't worry about anything, but in everything, through prayer and petition with thanksgiving, present your requests to God. And the peace of God, which surpasses all understanding, will guard your hearts and minds in Christ Jesus.

Philippians 4:4-7

Spend some time looking over your family's calendar, school agendas, and other to-do lists. Remember, you don't have to say yes to every invitation this season. Where can you cut back so that your teen can spend time celebrating the peace God promised in sending His Son? Consider blocking off time for your family to rest by doing something simple you can enjoy together, like baking, decorating the tree, or watching a Christmas movie. When we set aside time to rest and keep our focus on Christ this season, we can put many of our worries in the proper perspective.

MAKE A
PEACEFUL JAR

by Bekah Stoneking

Are there things that scare you or make you nervous? Is it sometimes hard to stop worrying about those things? Know today that God doesn't want us to be afraid. He tells us over and over in His Word, "Don't be afraid." The good news is that we don't have to rely on ourselves to find peace. Because of Jesus, we can have peace and find reasons to rejoice and celebrate, even during tough times.

GATHER

Gather your art supplies and work with your family to make a Peaceful Jar. You will need: a mixing bowl; a whisk; hot water; food coloring; clear school glue; fine glitter; a jar; twine; a tag; a miniature evergreen tree; and a permanent marker.

DIRECTIONS

Pour one part glue and four parts hot water, along with a few drops of food coloring, and as much glitter as you want into your mixing bowl. Use the whisk to mix your ingredients as hard as you can. Have a competition with your family to see who can whisk the fastest! Once your mixture is well blended, pour it into the jar. Hot glue the miniature evergreen tree to the bottom of the jar and let it dry. Then, put the lid on tightly (glue it into place if you'd like). Use the permanent marker to write the words to a Bible verse about peace—like Philippians 4:7—on the side of your jar or on a label/tag. When you are stressed, nervous, or scared, shake up your Peaceful Jar. Watch as the swirling glitter calms and settles while you practice reading and memorizing the Bible verse you wrote on the jar. Pray and ask God to remind you of the peace Jesus brings.

Later, when your friends need peace, share the Bible verse with them. When you are walking or driving around in your community and see hurting people, hear sirens, or see something frightening, pray for God's peace and protection to help the people in need. Celebrate the peace of Jesus this Christmas by sharing His peace with everyone, everywhere you go!

JOY

WEEK 3

FALL ON YOUR KNEES

by Elizabeth Hyndman

When we experience hope fulfilled and the dawn of peace, we worship in joyous celebration. Advent is a time of waiting, but it's also a time of great joy and celebration. We have the privilege of looking back, of remembering when our Savior and Messiah came to earth to redeem us and make all things new!

The shepherds' role in the Christmas story is one of action. They went from minding their flocks to investigating the good news of the angels to telling everyone to glorify and praise the Lord. When we encounter good news of this magnitude, we react.

The next line in the Christmas carol sings, "Fall on your knees! O hear the angels' voices."[1] I don't know that the shepherds fell on their knees—the Bible doesn't say that specifically. But I can imagine it would be impossible not to physically react to the news they'd just been told and the sights they saw.

We have the same good news today. The angel brought news of great joy:

> Don't be afraid, for look,
> I proclaim to you good
> news of great joy that will
> be for all the people.
>
> *Luke 2:10*

The good news of a Savior, a Messiah, Jesus Christ being born on earth is good news of great joy.

Even greater is the news we know now—that Jesus was born to live a perfect life on earth while teaching, healing, and performing miracles. That He died an excruciating death for our sins. And that three days later He rose from the dead, proving He was Lord over it. We know all this "according to the Scriptures" (1 Cor. 15:3-4).

That is the good news of great joy.

So we fall to our knees in worship, praising and glorifying God like the shepherds so long ago. Our Savior has come!

This week, we'll celebrate the coming of the Son of God to earth. We'll study about the Source of joy, how it can exist even in the midst of sorrow and pain, and how we can be bearers of joy through service and our lives. Together, let's worship the One the angels declared and the shepherds rushed to see.

We're to be people of great joy because we know the good news!

What from last week's personal study was particularly impactful for you?

Looking back over your life, what have been the most joy-filled times?

Most of us tend to equate joy with good circumstances. Perhaps some of our most joy-filled times include the day we got married, had our children, graduated from college, or landed our first job. But do you think it's possible to have joy in the midst of pain?

In the upside-down way of the kingdom, joy is a result of our suffering and our service. Can you describe a time when your suffering or service brought you joy?

Close your time in prayer, asking God to renew your understanding of what joy is. Pray for Him to open your eyes to see His gift of joy even in suffering and service.

JOY IN OUR SHEPHERD'S CARE

by Kelly D. King

First, read Psalm 23:1.

I still remember receiving my first cell phone on Christmas morning several years ago. At that time a cell phone was an extravagant gift. My husband, Vic, secretly placed the phone among the branches of our tree. As our family finished opening gifts, an unfamiliar ring came from inside the tree. I was baffled by the unexpected sound. As one who isn't often surprised, I was thrilled my husband pulled it off. It was an unexpected gift but greatly valued. It was a sacrifice to our monthly budget and an extravagance for our young family living on a single income. Since that year, the phone has been upgraded, replaced, and isn't viewed as an extravagance anymore, but rather a necessity.

I've also had disappointments on Christmas morning, or rather unmet expectations—like the first Christmas we were married and I opened my present to find jumper cables for my car. Vic still hasn't lived that one down. While I've experienced both happiness and disappointments on Christmas morning, I've realized two things—expectations can be an idol, and joy is not based on my circumstances but in the choice to live in God's extravagant grace.

The first Christmas in Bethlehem also had unmet expectations and unexpected circumstances. Joseph didn't expect a baby, and Mary definitely didn't expect a manger. Giving birth far from home, this young couple—even in their unforeseen, and possibly unwanted circumstances—experienced the joy of new birth. Visited by shepherds from the surrounding area, Mary must have remembered the words she sang as recorded in Luke 1:47—"My spirit rejoices in God my Savior." A song of joy. Joy was found in Bethlehem.

> Can you remember a time when you had unmet expectations? How did you respond?

In Luke 2, a host of angels announced the arrival of Jesus to a group of shepherds. This wasn't the first time God used shepherds in His plan. King David was selected to rule over Israel, and he was a shepherd boy. Many Old Testament heroes—including Abraham, Isaac, Jacob, Moses, and Amos—were also shepherds at one point. Even women shared in this lowly occupation. Genesis 29:9 describes Rachel as "a shepherdess."

Some of Israel's greatest men and women worked among fields full of smelly and vulnerable sheep.

Shepherds carried important responsibilities for their assigned flock. Some of these duties included protection, provision, and presence. Shepherds protected their herd from wild animals and the harsh environment, and they helped guide their sheep safely home. Shepherds provided for their sheep, ensuring they had plenty to eat and drink. Often shepherds would carry a small pail with them, filling it several times when sheep were unable to reach the stream. The shepherd's presence provided comfort—a place where sheep knew their shepherd's voice and could rest in his presence.

Just as shepherds perform these tasks for their sheep, the Lord does the same for those who follow Him.

READ PSALM 23. CONSIDER FOR A MOMENT HOW THE LORD HAS BEEN YOUR SHEPHERD.

How has the Lord protected you?

How has the Lord provided for you?

How have you experienced the Lord's presence?

Do you sometimes question why God has placed you in your current situation or occupation? How can you still find joy in your unmet expectations or unfilled desires?

Take a few minutes to pray Psalm 23 out loud as a way to express joy no matter what your circumstance might currently be. Read each phrase and turn it into a prayer of praise and thanksgiving.

READ 2 SAMUEL 6:12-22.

David wanted the ark of the covenant to be returned to Jerusalem, the nation's spiritual center. The ark represented God's presence among the people, and when it was brought back to Jerusalem, David's response in verse 14 was one of worship, dancing, and great joy.

Psalm 96 was written during the time when the ark was returned to Jerusalem.

Read Psalm 96 and underline verses that describe how we find joy in worship or write them in the margin here.

How do you express joy when you worship?

C. S. Lewis wrote,

The most obvious fact about praise—whether of God or anything—strangely escaped me ... I had never noticed that all enjoyment spontaneously overflows into praise.[2]

GOD CAN USE THE MOST UNEXPECTED CIRCUMSTANCES FOR HIS GLORY AND HE CAN USE YOU TO BE A MESSENGER OF JOY IN THIS SEASON.

What I love about David is that, through the Psalms especially, we see he was able to find joy in the Lord when he was in a pit of loss, anguish, and depression. David was also able to find joy in the Lord when victories and miraculous answers to prayer abounded. David's joy overflowed out of his heart for the Lord. Circumstances didn't dictate his joy or his faith in God.

> How have you seen your joy in the Lord waver during difficult seasons? How can you maintain joy even when life isn't meeting your expectations?

> As you prepare your heart for Christmas morning, how are you approaching the day with expectations? How will you respond if those expectations aren't met? How will you choose to celebrate Christ and find joy in knowing He is the Good Shepherd?

A joy-giver is confident in the Lord, content, likes being around positive people, seeks to be obedient to the Lord, enjoys celebrations, and rests in the Lord's plan for her life.

A joy-taker exhibits self-pity, focuses on comparison, is a complainer, is a negative influence, is overcommitted, and is even constantly exhausted.

> Which one best describes you? Are you a joy-giver or a joy-taker?

> What changes do you need to make to live with joy?

Let's choose to cultivate joy in our lives despite our circumstances, because we know that our Shepherd is caring for us every step of the way.

JOY MAY COME THROUGH SUFFERING

by Emily Chadwell

First, read Hebrews 12:1–2.

Several years ago, my family traveled to Jackson Hole, Wyoming, for Christmas. One of the highlights of our trip was snowmobiling through Yellowstone National Park.

During a stop on our excursion, our tour guide said something that has stuck with me. He was telling us about the fire in Yellowstone in 1988, which covered 1.2 million acres. People were terrified that one of America's greatest national parks had been permanently damaged. But then our guide said something remarkable—while most people were panicking, experts in the field knew that fire was a necessary part of the park's growth. They knew that in order for Yellowstone to continue to produce life, it first had to die. And that's exactly what happened.

When I heard this, Jesus' words in John's Gospel came to mind: "Unless a grain of wheat falls to the ground and dies, it remains by itself. But if it dies, it produces much fruit" (12:24). Jesus was talking about more than gardening, of course. He was shedding light on the upside-down nature of His kingdom, where life comes out of death and joy comes out of suffering.

We live in a culture that wrongfully believes God helps those who help themselves. We think that if we do the right thing, we'll earn a life of comfort; but if we do the wrong thing, we'll earn a life of suffering. In the upside-down way of the kingdom, though, suffering isn't merely a form of punishment reserved for the disobedient. In fact, Scripture is clear that the obedient will suffer, and that their suffering is actually a sign of their status as children of God.

READ 1 PETER 2:18–25.

According to verse 20b, what brings favor from God?

Why are we called to suffer for doing good (v. 21)?

Can you remember a time when your obedience brought suffering? How did you react?

Even as Christians we can easily fall into the trap of thinking that our obedience entitles us to pain-free life. Too often we're like the older brother in the parable of the prodigal son (Luke 15:11-32), who thought his perfect record entitled him to certain privileges. He was furious when, upon his reckless and disobedient younger brother's homecoming, his father threw a massive party. His father had never thrown *him* a party, and he had done everything right!

What are the dangers in comparing your suffering to someone else's suffering (or seeming lack thereof)?

Jesus shatters any notion that a perfect life exempts us from suffering. He was without sin, and yet He suffered far more than any other.

READ HEBREWS 5:7-9.

According to verse 8, what did Jesus learn? How did He learn it?

Being God's Son didn't disqualify Jesus from suffering. In fact, His suffering qualified Him to be our High Priest, who is able to "sympathize with our weaknesses" because He was tempted in every way that we are and yet He never sinned (Heb. 4:15).

We also see from this passage the clear connection between obedience and suffering—as we suffer, we learn to obey God just as Jesus did. However, when the author of Hebrews wrote about Jesus learning obedience, he didn't mean Jesus had to overcome disobedience like we do. Rather, by saying that Jesus learned obedience he means Jesus continually said yes to God's will every day, culminating with the crucifixion.[3]

This is important to take notice of. The life of faith is a daily walk of obedience and trust. Christians do ourselves a disservice when we wait until our lives are falling apart to finally get serious about our faith. Spiritual disciplines (prayer, reading the Word, Christian fellowship, and so forth) aren't meant to act as an emergency surgery—an immediate and necessary reaction in crisis to prevent the worst possible scenario. Rather, they are daily practices we engage in to prepare us for what's ahead.

Jesus modeled a life of daily faith as, every day, in a million ways, He submitted Himself to the will of the Father. When He prayed in the garden of Gethsemane, "Yet not as I will, but as you will" (Matt. 26:39b), that wasn't the first time He laid down His will. Each daily act of obedience leading up to that prepared Him for obedience at the cross.

> Can you identify a situation in your life when God called you to obey Him in small ways in order to prepare you to obey Him in a much larger way down the road? Explain.

THANKFULLY, THE OBEDIENT AREN'T CALLED TO SUFFER JUST FOR SUFFERING'S SAKE. GOD'S END GOAL IS OUR JOY.

READ HEBREWS 12:1-2.

According to verse 2, why did Jesus endure the cross?

In the upside-down kingdom of God, obedience goes hand-in-hand with suffering, and suffering goes hand-in-hand with joy. Jesus' obedience led Him to the cross, and Jesus endured the cross for the joy set before Him—being in the presence of God.[4] The good news for us is, because Jesus came to the earth and offered His life as a sacrifice for us, we have access to the Father here and now, in whose "presence is abundant joy" (Ps. 16:11). What's more, we have the Spirit of Christ in us, who causes the fruit of joy to overflow in us as we walk in step with Him (Gal. 5:22).

> Read the following verses, jotting down what each one says about suffering and joy.

- Psalm 30:5b

- John 16:21-22

- Romans 5:3-5

- 1 Peter 4:12-13

In the article "The Joy We Know Only in Suffering," Marshall Segal wrote,

> God can build a blazing and refreshing sanctuary in the wilderness. He turns our deserts into places for us to explore and express greater depths of delight in him. Instead of being a threat to real joy, he often makes our suffering a means to even more.[5]

> Can you think of a time in your life when you found your greatest joy in your deepest suffering? Explain.

It can be tempting to base our joy on our circumstances, but the apostle Paul wrote from a prison cell,

> Rejoice in the Lord always. I will say it again: Rejoice!
>
> *Philippians 4:4*

Always. That means when things are going better than planned or worse than imagined, we're to have joy in the Lord. How? In the wise words of Elisabeth Elliot,

The secret is Christ in me, not me in a different set of circumstances.[6]

Read James 1:2-4 below and journal what you've learned today about joy and suffering.

Consider it a great joy, my brothers and sisters, whenever you experience various trials, because you know that the testing of your faith produces endurance. And let endurance have its full effect, so that you may be mature and complete, lacking nothing.

James 1:2-4

SERVE WITH JOY!

by Debbie Dickerson

First, read John 13:4-5; Philippians 2:5-11; and 1 Peter 5:2-5.

Three little letters ribboned together tingle from the Christmas tree, glitter in the snow globe, and serenade us with songs this wondrous season. The letter J swirls as if set to music and twirls the letter O. The two then bow to make a Y, and JOY curtsies in our soul. When the lights are dimmed, the confetti has fallen, and the last note is played, joy longs for an encore. But how do we keep joy dancing in our souls once the decorations are tucked away in the attic? The tinsel gone, we're sure there's more to joy than just the glitter.

Our souls know joy is in the holy that has come down—with a love song that never ends. Perhaps you've celebrated Jesus' birth for years, but joy has become a silent partner. Perhaps you're meeting Jesus for the first time. However you've arrived this Advent season, will you prepare your heart and join me on bended knees? It's where Jesus will lead us best.

> Read Philippians 2:5-11 like a slow dance with the Holy Spirit. Ask Him to speak the words into your soul so that when you rise, you may "adopt the same attitude as that of Christ Jesus" (v. 5).

Why did Jesus come, and how does His coming bring us unending joy? We experience joy as we become more Christlike. So, what is this attitude of Christ we are supposed to adopt? The answer is actually set to music in verses 6-11 as God inspired Paul to share the words of a hymn most likely written before his time or perhaps by him. Like a lullaby, the words sing of the coming of Jesus from the only-imaginable heaven to the all-too-real earth.

Think of it: Baby Jesus, "who, existing in the form of God, did not consider equality with God as something to be exploited. Instead he emptied himself by assuming the form of a servant, taking on the likeness of humanity" (Phil. 2:6-7a). Fully God, fully man, the Babe of Bethlehem. Through His incarnation, Jesus willingly and joyfully set aside some of His rights as the Divine and took on the limitations of human nature with thoughts and feelings like ours, yet all without sin. When we give thought to Jesus' heavenly life before His earthly birth, His emptying Himself reveals the greater depth of His selfless love for us. This doctrine—*kenosis*, from the Greek word describing Christ's emptying Himself[7]—is our introduction to our Savior today. And there He lay: Immanuel in a manger.

> What do we need to empty ourselves of in order to serve others more joyfully and humbly?

In Matthew 20:28, Jesus explained, "the Son of Man did not come to be served, but to serve." He did the incredible and literally assumed "the form of a servant" (Phil. 2:7a). From this we see both the outer shape of His humanity and the inner nature of His selflessness. We, too, have the outer shape of humanity, but is our inner nature servant-shaped or self-shaped?

Let's fast-forward to the end of Jesus' earthly ministry and stay on our knees to try to imagine one of the most tender moments when He showed us how to live as a servant.

READ JOHN 13:3-5.

Immanuel unveiled Himself. A towel, not a robe. A basin, not a scepter. The reversal of roles could not be ignored. The Divine bent His holy knees and slipped the dusty sandals from the feet of each disciple. Here on the very night before Jesus would suffer and die on the cross, we see Him even washing the feet of the one whom He knew would betray Him. Perhaps it is at this expression that we cover our gasping mouths at the measure of His love. And surely we sigh when we see our own feet in His hands and realize that we, too, at one time were His enemies. But shall we remain speechless at the thought of adopting this same attitude of Christ?

Not if we're asking for an encore of joy. Our cue comes from the reversal of roles. In our self-shaped nature, serving doesn't feel fulfilling. But when we adopt the attitude of Christ and empty ourselves of our rights, we take on a servant form and find we are filled with joy just as Jesus promises: "Truly I tell you, a servant is not greater than his master. ... If you know these things, you are blessed if you do them" (John 13:16-17). Blessed, happy. Can't you imagine how Jesus enjoyed amazing the Twelve with this loving gesture?

Have you ever experienced a time when serving others brought you great—maybe even unexpected—joy? What were the circumstances?

The tone now set for the crescendo of His service, Jesus "humbled himself by becoming obedient to the point of death—even to death on a cross" (Phil. 2:8). Jesus knew He is the only hope for our salvation. So, humbly, obediently, and "for the joy that lay before him" (Heb. 12:2), He gave Himself for us. What a striking chord of love! The climax for His coming resounded in His resurrection and ascension to the Father, as He defeated sin and death for those who would trust in Him.

> For this reason God highly exalted him and gave him the name that is above every name, so that at the name of Jesus every knee will bow—in heaven and on earth and under the earth—and every tongue will confess that Jesus Christ is Lord, to the glory of God the Father.
>
> *Philippians 2:9-11*

ON OUR KNEES IS WHERE WE STARTED IN PRAYER. ON OUR KNEES IS WHERE WE'LL STAY IN SERVICE. AND ON OUR KNEES IS WHERE WE'LL SING OF THE HOLY ONE WHO HAS COME. THEREIN IS THE ENCORE—JOY IN BECOMING MORE CHRISTLIKE AS WE SERVE, AND JOY IN KNOWING HE IS OUR ULTIMATE REWARD.

C. S. Lewis realized,

> God cannot give us a happiness and peace apart from Himself, because it is not there. There is no such thing.[8]

As Christ followers, let's disrobe ourselves of our self-centered rights, clothing ourselves instead "with humility toward one another" (1 Pet. 5:5).

> How can you serve others this Advent season and share the love of Christ by extending yourself with simple gestures? List specific ideas below.

Pray for opportunities to show the attitude of Christ even in the inconveniences of your day. May joy keep you light on your feet as you slip your hand into His and let Jesus take the lead.

JOY COMES IN THE PRESENCE OF JESUS

by Emma Wilson

First, read Psalm 16:11 and Luke 2:15.

Almost exactly this time a year ago, I was walking down the aisle to the man of my dreams. That December day was truly the greatest day of my life to date, and by some miracle, everything seemed to come together flawlessly.

Since the moment I got engaged, I prayed fervently for an unusually warm day for our outdoor ceremony, and I woke up to find a forecast of 55°F. All of our loved ones were there, witnessing our marriage form before their eyes. And, most importantly, we had a table that was filled with every flavor of cake pop I could dream up. I was the happiest I'd ever been.

While that day was more perfect than I had even hoped, it came and went in the blink of an eye. Next thing I knew, I was beginning a sometimes mundane life with my new husband, having left my family, friends, and everything I'd previously known to start this journey with him.

On paper, marriage honestly seems like a bit of an unfair trade. Seriously, think about it. Why would you want to leave the freedoms of singlehood, the ability to craft your life the way you'd like without having to worry about the schedule and preferences of another person, and potentially have to leave the life and people you already know and love, all to be bound to this one person forever? If you're engaged or married, then you know why.

Personal preferences are an easy sacrifice for the unexplainable joy you feel in living life with your spouse. Not because your marriage looks glamorous in any way, or because you're happy all the time, or because you or your husband are the perfect spouse. But because of the love of simply being with your teammate.

This is only a taste of what we have in Jesus, only a dimly lit picture of the fullness of life we find in the manger. As believers, you and I can experience unwavering joy every day by experiencing the presence of Jesus through His Word.

READ LUKE 2:15-16.

Flash. Angels. Glory. Fear. Something strange appeared in the shepherds' field, shaking up their nightly routine, and what they were seeing wasn't making a lick of sense.

Back in verse 10, the angels saw the shepherds' fear and, in effect, said, *Hey guys, it's OK! We come bringing joy. And it's for everybody—including you. For Christ, whom you've been waiting for—He's here!* The angels broke out into heavenly praise right before the shepherds' eyes. And then, just as quickly as they came, the angels went.

I've got to admit, I don't think any Christmas light show is going to be able to outdo what the shepherds experienced.

> What would you do if you had witnessed all of that? Don't think about it too hard. What's your first instinct?

Mine would probably be to gather up my sheep, put them somewhere safe for the night, and sit alone in shock, thinking, *I've gone absolutely bonkers.* I'd try to pretend it never happened and recover as best as I could.

Unbelievably, that's not at all what these shepherds did. One of them looked at the others, and, full of faith that what they'd just heard was true, he said, *We've got to go to Bethlehem and see this.*

Wait, what? That's some bold belief, because going came with consequences. Going meant their sheep might be lost or killed. They could lose their work, their living. Everyone they talked to about it would call them lunatics until the end of time. And yet, not only did they go—they "hurried off" (v. 16).

There was another shepherd, hundred of years before their time, who would have understood what these shepherds in the Book of Luke were experiencing.

READ PSALM 16.

In Psalm 16:2, David wrote, "I said to the LORD, 'You are my Lord; I have nothing good besides you.'"

We know, based on David's tone throughout the psalm, that he was going through a difficult season. He asked for protection (v. 1) and mentioned his troubling thoughts as he fell asleep each night (v. 7). But none of these difficulties was his focus. In essence, David was saying in verse 2, "Yahweh, You are my Master because in You is everything, and it is better than life itself to be Yours."

David finished this song of worship by proclaiming to the Lord, "in your presence is abundant joy; at your right hand are eternal pleasures" (v. 11). Both David and the shepherds of Luke 2 believed in their God, went into His presence with haste, and found fullness of joy in the only place it could truly be found.

> How would you describe your belief in God? Bold? Timid? Life-altering? Distracted? Are you convinced, like David and the shepherds, that joy comes from being with God?

Sometimes, belief is easier to claim when it requires only my mind and not my life. It's easy to say I'm satisfied in Christ while I look to people, success, and worldly comforts to give me joy.

But there is no joy apart from Christ. God knew that, and because He loved us so much, He sent His Son to the earth as a sacrifice so that we could experience eternal joy in His presence.

Choosing to find joy in Christ and not in what the world offers can be hard. Hurrying off to spend time in His presence when the world is full of so many appealing distractions is challenging. I think of Martha, who couldn't seem to leave her everyday tasks to be with Jesus. But her sister, Mary, sat at Jesus' feet, listening to and learning from Him. Jesus said, "Mary has chosen what is better, and it will not be taken away from her" (Luke 10:42, NIV).

The good portion. The only thing worth having. Martha chose other things, remaining unsatisfied, while her joy sat right in her living room.

> What do you have trouble leaving in order to spend time with Jesus? What distracts you from finding abundant joy in Christ?

WHEN THE SHEPHERDS LEFT EVERYTHING AND TOOK OFF TO BETHLEHEM, THEY WENT FULL OF FAITH THAT WHAT—OR WHO—THEY WOULD FIND WOULD BE BETTER THAN EVERYTHING THEY'D LEFT BEHIND. AND THEY DIDN'T COME BACK DISAPPOINTED.

Do you struggle with experiencing the presence of Jesus in the midst of our culture's take on Christmas?

How can you be mindful of God's presence today—at work, at home, at church?

How can you extend this season's celebration and joy beyond Advent?

C. S. Lewis wrote in *Mere Christianity*, "Look for Christ, and you will find Him. And with Him, everything else."[9] Look for Him first. Choose Him this Christmas season. And when you do, you will find eternal pleasures and joy in abundance.

JOY IS CONTAGIOUS

by Leigh Ann Dans

First, read Luke 2:17–18.

Real joy always compels us to tell someone else what we have experienced.

Recently, one night around 6:30 p.m., my neighbors texted me three very scary words: "We are flooding." I ran to my back door and looked out, and sure enough, my backyard was a river. The creek behind my house had overflowed its banks. I could see police lights flashing across the street, where a car was stranded in the rising flood. Muddy water was creeping up the side of my new HVAC unit beneath my back deck. One of my worst fears was being realized as the creek continued to rise.

The next day, as I sat watching the continuing rain, I struggled with fear. *What if I have to replace my HVAC unit? What if the creek overflows again?* As I worried, I heard the Lord whisper to my heart, "That creek is My creek and this house is My house. I live here, too." God was reminding me that He is *here* with me, always. What do I have to fear? He was asking me to put my trust in Him and take joy in His ability to handle a rising creek. Joy and peace flooded my soul as I trusted my good Father to care for me, His beloved child.

A few days later I held a prayer meeting at my house and told my small group what happened. They prayed over me and my house, and we all prayed over the creek. One person specifically asked God to bless my house and land by cleaning the creek that runs behind my neighborhood.

Because of the joy and peace in my heart, and the confidence I had in my Father to take care of me, I made the decision to tell several neighbors that our creek had been prayed over. I gave witness that my God is a creek cleaner and that I was trusting Him to take care of us. I also shared with them how He was cleansing me of my fears and taking me to a deeper level of trust in Him as He lifted my heart and restored my joy.

Four days after that prayer meeting, the local water department contacted our neighborhood and told us they would be coming to clean out the creek!

I've lived in my neighborhood for fifteen years and have experienced other floods, but this was the first time any promise was made to clean the creek out.

READ PSALM 126.

When God brought His people out of captivity and restored their fortunes, they were so happy they felt like they were living in a dream! What did their joy propel them to do?

When God does a work in our lives—answers prayer, comforts us with His presence, and makes His power known—we can't help but to be filled with the joy that comes from knowing He is who He says He is. The natural response to that joy is to share the good news! I felt confident in telling my neighbors about what my group had prayed for, even though I had no idea when the answer would come. I simply recognized the opportunity to give a witness and open the door for them to know what I believed.

When I think of Christ's coming I don't limit it to His birth. When I see the baby figurine lying in my nativity scene during Christmastime, I'm reminded of that night when He came, but I'm also reminded that He is with me today and every day. The testimony of His work in my life is not something that happened years ago the day I became a Christian; rather, His work in me is a living, breathing, growing testimony. It is a story of what He has done in my life and a story of what He is doing right now.

Think about your salvation story. How has God continued to change you and do a work in your life since that day?

READ LUKE 2:17-18.

Don't you know that what those shepherds saw and heard on that first Christmas night built their faith? It might have even been their first introduction to God and His plan to bring a Messiah into the world. And they were so overjoyed they couldn't keep the news to themselves! They shared the joy of how God had made Himself known to them.

The shepherds are just one biblical example of people who experienced joy when God moved on their behalf. For example, Sarah, Hannah, and Elizabeth were all women who were unable to have children, until God moved. Their pregnancies were great cause for celebration because God made the impossible possible.

> Read the stories of Sarah, Hannah, and Elizabeth, and try to imagine the joy and gratitude they felt for their pregnancies. Jot down a few notes about how each of these women reacted to God's work in their lives.
>
> Sarah—Genesis 18:9-15; 21:1-7
>
>
>
> Hannah—1 Samuel 1–2
>
>
>
> Elizabeth—Luke 1:5-25

I'm leaving soon to travel with my grandson to El Salvador to share the love of Christ with the people there. I want them and my grandson to know the joy that is in my heart because Jesus has come into my life. I have a testimony of the day He saved me, and I have an ongoing testimony of the joy of experiencing Him in my life moment by moment as He shows me His love and miraculous power all the time.

> In what ways is God working in and through you right now during this season that you can share with others?

HOW CAN YOU BE A BEARER OF JOY TODAY?

LEARN FAUX CALLIGRAPHY

FOR GIFT TAGS AND CARDS

by Larissa Arnault Roach

The gifts must get wrapped, so why not turn this into a night of fun and celebration? Invite your besties, small group Bible study friends, or a few work buddies over for a night of learning how to hand letter. If you're sending Christmas cards, you can use your new skills there as well!

GATHER

- Pens, pencils, markers, and crayons
- Scrap paper for practicing
- Gift tags

DIRECTIONS

Start with a short lesson. If someone in your group is already good at calligraphy or hand-lettering, have her instruct! If not, watch a couple YouTube® videos together and get out some practice sheets.

Faux calligraphy uses any standard writing instrument, so you don't need a fancy dip pen. Use the examples on the facing page to get started, or download copies of our free printables at lifeway.com/adventstudy for easy tracing.

As you write each recipient's name on a tag, pray for her. Pray for her to experience joy this holiday season, and pray for her to be continually pointed back to Christ.

You could also turn this party up a notch and make it a full-on gift wrapping affair. Ask everyone to bring two rolls of wrapping paper, scissors, tape, gift bags, and embellishments (think candy canes, ribbon of all kinds, baker's twine, ornaments, greenery from your yard or Christmas tree, washi tape, stamps, and whatever craft supplies you have on hand).

Share ideas, mix and match paper and bows, and set off each wrapped gift with the special tags you've created.

FIND JOY IN GIVING
YOUR TIME

by Karen Daniel

There are a lot of things for your teens to look forward to this time of year. They get a break from school, there are parties to attend, and there are gifts to give and to receive. But the joy we get from these things is often circumstantial; it's here today and gone tomorrow.

You KonMari your home all morning only to lose all those hard-earned "sparks of joy"[10] as soon as your son walks in the door and launches his dirty gym bag down the hallway. You pick up your daughter on the last day of school before the break, both of you excited to get home and begin decorating the house and baking cookies, when out of nowhere she gets a text that puts that all-too-familiar "I don't want to talk about it" look on her face again. Nope, circumstantial joy just doesn't cut it.

Print Luke 2:10-11 and hang it on your fridge, or write it out on a decorative chalkboard. Place it somewhere your family will see it all season long.

The joy God gives us in Jesus isn't restricted to our circumstances. In fact, when we experience the joy of Christ it naturally begins to overflow into praise.

> Suddenly there was a multitude of the heavenly host with the angel, praising God and saying: Glory to God in the highest heaven, and peace on earth to people he favors!
>
> *Luke 2:13-14*

Notice, too, that the angels didn't make God's grand announcement of the Messiah to the local government or priests. They proclaimed Jesus' birth to shepherds in a field.

God often works in unexpected ways for His glory, and He can use us to be messengers of joy in this season. It can be as simple as saying Merry Christmas to the clerk at the store or packing Samaritan's Purse shoeboxes of simple toys and necessities for children who wouldn't otherwise have what they need.[11] Or perhaps volunteering as a family to participate in a local toy drive. Let your teen experience the joy of not just purchasing toys for less fortunate children this year but being available to hand them out when the time comes.

MAKE

PRAISE ART

by Bekah Stoneking

Since the moment sin entered the world, God's people have been waiting for Him to send the Messiah to rescue them. For thousands of years, they waited. And now we're waiting again for Christ's return.

Has it been easy for you to be patient and wait for Christmas? Are you starting to get frustrated with waiting? This feeling might help you imagine how God's people felt as they waited for Jesus to come. But in the midst of their waiting, they still found reasons to praise God. King David wrote many poems and praise songs because he was full of joy from the Lord. We have some of his poetry in our Bibles!

In Psalm 23, David wrote that because God is like a good shepherd, God's sheep—people like you and me—are taken care of, are loved, and have everything they need. God cares for you so much! On hard days and on good days, God is taking care of us. His love for us is unending. In fact, God loves us so much He sent Jesus. People who trust Jesus to rescue them from their sin are filled with hope, peace, and joy from God, Himself. This is a great reason to celebrate and praise God!

Practice opening your Bible to the Book of Psalms. Read Psalm 23 with your family. Try to read the words in a rhythm or make up hand motions to help you remember the verses.

Use colorful markers to write words from Psalm 23 or other words of praise onto construction paper. Decorate the papers using Christmas stickers, glitter, stamps, and other supplies. Deliver your artwork to your neighbors' homes or mail them to your friends to spread Christmas joy.

While you are making your praise art, consider making a card inviting someone who may miss her family—like a single or elderly person from your church or a new neighbor—to come to your house to decorate for Christmas and celebrate Jesus with your family.

LOVE

WEEK 4

O NIGHT DIVINE

by Elizabeth Hyndman

This week, we finally get to the moment we've been waiting for, longing for, hoping for. This week Christmas comes. We look back and remember that first Christmas, when God demonstrated His love for us by sending His Son to be with us on earth.

We sing, "O night divine, O night, when Christ was born!"[1]

From Genesis 3 until Matthew 2, all of history waited for this moment. Eve, Abraham, Rahab, Naomi, David, Isaiah, Malachi, Anna, and Simeon waited for the Messiah to come to their rescue. They waited for a Savior and a Redeemer.

The Child born on that divine night came to save us all. He is the Christ. He came to save us, to redeem us, and to demonstrate once and for all the way God loves us.

Every year we celebrate the love of God on Christmas. We reflect on His love for us, and we strive to demonstrate His love to others. We give gifts, make food, pray, worship, and serve with and for one another.

We observe Advent in part so that Christmas will be all the more meaningful. We know and appreciate God's love all the more through the perspective of waiting and hoping. We can better enjoy the Light if we've been through the dark.

As we celebrate the love of God this week, we'll also take time to understand how a God like ours can love a people like us. We'll learn how God demonstrated and still demonstrates His love for us. We'll respond together in action and wonder.

We pray you know the wonder of hope, peace, joy, and love this Advent season. We pray as we close these pages that we will be people who are bearers of that same hope, peace, joy, and love to the world around us.

"Sweet hymns of joy in grateful chorus raise we;
Let all within us praise His holy name.
Christ is the Lord! O praise His name forever!
His power and glory evermore proclaim!"[2]

What from last week's personal study was particularly impactful for you?

Describe an experience when you felt greatly loved. What did that love compel you to do?

God loved us so much He gave us His Son. Love compels us to give—time, resources, affirming words, and so forth. How do you see this truth play out in your life?

How has the wonder of God's love transformed your life? What actions do you take to share this love with others?

As you close in prayer, thank God for His immeasurable love in sending Jesus to the earth so we could be reconciled to Him. Ask Him to help you show that love to others.

GOD LOVED, GOD GAVE

by Amanda Mae Steele

First, read John 3:16-17.

At Christmastime many of us look forward to buying the perfect gifts for our friends and family. Some of us may enjoy receiving more than giving, but giver and receiver alike both agree that a meaningful gift has the powerful potential to communicate love and appreciation.

I think it's safe to say that the greater the love we have for someone (regardless of whether or not it's Christmas), the more lavishly we are willing to spend on or sacrifice for them: a young man saving up the equivalent of many months of his salary so he can propose to the girl he loves with a beautiful ring; a mother and father who sacrifice their own dreams and work multiple jobs to put their children through college; and so on.

Yet there's no worldly comparison to the most valuable gift ever given in the history of mankind. It is the gift of life—and not just life on this earth, but life everlasting in the presence of God. This gift has no monetary value; instead, it was paid for with the currency of pain, suffering, and blood—the only worthy payment for an impossible price tag.

Our text today is one that might be very familiar to you. Many young children and newer Christians are encouraged to memorize this verse early on in their faith. You might even find it on a Forever 21® shopping bag or on an In-N-Out Burger® drink cup! But there's a good reason John 3:16 has essentially been the most popular verse of the Bible: it sums up the gospel in a nutshell.

> For God loved the world in this way: He gave his one and only Son, so that everyone who believes in him will not perish but have eternal life.
>
> *JOHN 3:16*

How did God show His love for the world?

Why did He do that?

Simple enough, right? As maturing Christians, we cannot hit the fast-forward button on familiar passages and assume we know everything there is to know about them. We continually need to dig deeper into God's living and breathing Word with great expectation that the Holy Spirit will illuminate God's Word in a way we've never experienced before. Only then can we be captivated by awe and wonder at His faithfulness as we ponder the value of God's sacrificial gift to you and me.

What was your honest gut reaction when you read that the passage for today was John 3:16-17? What expectations did you have?

Verse 16 starts with a small word that should cause us to think twice when we read it: "for." Non-grammar nerds, please stick with me for a minute—"for" is a coordinating conjunction or a connector, meaning we need to track backward a little bit because we have a clue that this verse was not meant to stand alone. The common coordinating conjunctions to watch out for in the Bible include:

- For
- And
- Nor
- But
- Or
- Yet
- So

You can remember these coordinating conjunctions by remembering "FANBOYS." (You're welcome for the handy mnemonic device!)

Context is extremely important to accurately interpret the Bible the way God intended for us to do, so let's take a few steps back and read John 3:14-15:

> Just as Moses lifted up the snake in the wilderness, so the Son of Man must be lifted up, so that everyone who believes in him may have eternal life.

John 3:14-15

To which character from the Old Testament did Jesus compare the Son of Man?

Who do you think Moses symbolizes?

Read Numbers 21. What happened when bitten people looked at the snake?

God has long been in the business of healing the sick even before Jesus appeared as the Son of Man. God has always wanted healing and wholeness for His children, but there was only one way for humanity to be fully healed and reconciled to God.

READ JOHN 3:17.

John 3:17 may be a less familiar verse than John 3:16, but I think many people would find greater comfort if they read John 3:16-17 together. It's as if Jesus is reassuring us that God's motives really are good and that He doesn't want us to fail. Jesus is telling us God's motive isn't to judge us as many people fear, but that God's heart is truly about saving us through Jesus—through His special *one and only* Son!

Insert your name in the spaces provided below, and then read it aloud:

"For God loved the world in this way: He gave his one and only Son, so that _____ who believes in him will not perish but have eternal life. For God did not send his Son into the world to condemn _____, but to save _____ through him."

There was no other atonement worthy of God's grace because God is matchless. The only One who could do it was Jesus. And God, knowing the pain of the sacrifice, yet valuing the outcome more, gave us the one gift that will never disappoint.

Open it, marvel at it, rejoice in it, and share it.

What's something new you discovered today in reading this passage?

Did anyone come to mind as you were studying this Scripture today? Pray and ask God to reveal who in your life needs to hear the good news and receive the gift of His Son, Jesus. Write their names here and pray for opportunities to talk to them about the gospel of Christ.

How might God be calling you to give the gift of Jesus to others this season?

Father God, I pray that my sister is renewed by reading Your Word today. Help her to slow down during the hustle and bustle of this season, that she may pause and remember Your promise that You did not send Jesus to condemn her but to save her. May she find joy, hope, and healing in the Son who paid the price, so that she could freely receive and enjoy your indescribable gift!

LOVE WAS GOD'S IDEA

by Rachel Forrest

First, read 1 John 4:7–12.

My daughter recently lost her first tooth. My husband and I, after some debate and discussion, decided we would do the whole Tooth Fairy thing and enabled that imaginative wonder for her. However, the wonder didn't last. Later on that day, my daughter asked, "Mommy, is the Tooth Fairy real?" Determined not to lie, I replied, "Well, what do you think?" She answered that she believed, but a friend from church told her the fairy tale wasn't real and that parents pretend to be the Tooth Fairy. My daughter then reasoned, "I know leprechauns and pots of gold aren't real, so I think the Tooth Fairy probably isn't real either."

I couldn't argue with her reasoning. Like me, she's a logical thinker. I like to see how things connect from one step to another, and I appreciate the reason behind the design. Whenever we go somewhere as a family, I often tell my children, "OK, this is the plan …" and I detail what we're going to do when we arrive. I like order and structure.

My need for order can make the holidays stressful. When we pull out the Christmas decorations from storage and prepare to decorate the tree, I start to feel my anxiety rise because I suffer from POPD—Perfect Ornament Placement Disorder—and decking the halls with two children under the age of six is anything but perfect. Decorating our tree looks more like chaos than order as my plans for a perfectly curated holiday experience meet the reality of my circumstances.

Maybe you can relate to the frustration that comes when things don't go according to plan. The good news is that the gospel is for those of us who find our plans displaced by a disappointing reality at Christmas. God is the author of order, not chaos, and the sending of His Son into the world was not an act of random happenstance. God planned it from the beginning of time; it is rooted in His loving and unchanging character.

Why do you think God sent Jesus to the world?

When we think about why God sent His Son into the world, we might conclude that it was because of sin. After all, it was John who proclaimed at the sight of Jesus, "Here is the Lamb of God, who takes away the sin of the world!" (John 1:29). John stated this again in no uncertain terms in his first epistle. He said, "God ... sent his Son to be the atoning sacrifice for our sins" (1 John 4:10). Redemption of sin is arguably a cause for God's decision to send Jesus into the world. Yet, there seems to be more at play here than just payment for sin.

In the ancient Greek world in which John wrote, philosophers had developed multiple views on causation, or the cause of an outcome. Two types of causation were the final cause and the efficient cause. The final cause is the purpose for which something is done, or the end that is hoped for. For example, you build a table for the purpose of dining at it. The efficient cause is that which causes change to happen, or simply the thing that brings something about. So, in our prior example, you're the cause because you're the thing creating changes that result in a table.[3]

From this perspective, we can see that John related two causes for why God sent His Son into the world. Look again at the passage in 1 John:

> God's love was revealed among us in this way: God sent his one
> and only Son into the world so that we might live through him.
> Love consists in this: not that we loved God, but that he loved
> us and sent his Son to be the atoning sacrifice for our sins.

> *1 John 4:9-10*

God sent His Son for the purpose of satisfying the penalty for sin and appeasing the holy wrath of the Father justly poured out on all unrighteousness. Atonement for sin was the final cause.

But don't miss this: John said that it was also love that sent Jesus into the world. Notice how he listed it first—"[God] loved us and sent his Son to be the atoning sacrifice for our sins" (v. 10).

God's love for His creation was the efficient cause. Love is rooted in the very character of God, which means it was, by nature, preexistent before sin entered the world. In other words, God initiated love long ago, from eternity past.

READ EPHESIANS 1:4 AND 2 TIMOTHY 1:9.

How do each of these passages prove the eternal nature of God's redemptive love?

Jesus' incarnation and atoning work on the cross was God's plan all along. We may think that God created the world and mankind in holy perfection and harmonious relationship with Him, but because of Eve's temptation and sin and Adam's subsequent fall into sin, God had to develop a new game plan to accommodate for His now-broken creation. But that is inconsistent with His character.

READ MALACHI 3:1 AND JAMES 1:17.

What do these verses say about God's nature?

In theology, this is known as God's immutability, and it means that God is unchanging. His love for us is unchanging, and it's this immutable, redemptive love, which existed before the foundation of the world, that led to Him sending His Son, Jesus, into the world to be the atoning sacrifice for our sin.

One of my favorite Christmas hymns is "Joy to the World! The Lord Is Come." The concluding lines to the song proclaim the wonders of God's love. The love of God is not a passive love. We don't receive it once at salvation and then move on from it.

Instead, John said,

> Dear friends, if God loved us in this way, we also must love one
> another. No one has ever seen God. If we love one another, God
> remains in us and his love is made complete in us.

> *1 John 4:11-12*

As we come to know our identity as chosen and loved in Jesus Christ, we're to
pour out that love to others.

> Do you know the unchanging, eternal love of God through Jesus, His
> Son? How can you share that love with others this Christmas?

LOVE IS ACTION

by Paige Clayton

First, read 1 John 3:16–18.

My father loved my mother very much, and he expressed his love by surprising her with sweet gifts. He died more than twenty years ago after a long battle with an unnamed degenerative neurological disease that slowly stole him away from us. The disease robbed him of his fine motor skills, his speech, and so much more.

When his speech was all but gone, he was still able to play some golf, which was one of his greatest joys on the earth. One day, when Mom picked him up from the golf course, my father looked very disheveled and more tired than usual. It took a long time of talking to him and the people he was with at the golf club to realize he hadn't played golf at all that day. Instead, he walked, shuffling a lot of the way, the two miles to and from a nearby mall to try to buy my mother a piece of jewelry for her birthday. Because his speech was virtually gone, he was unable to purchase what he wanted for her, so the surprise was ruined.

My mom didn't get a new piece of jewelry for her birthday that year, but the knowledge of that act of love, which came at great cost to my father's physical strength, was more precious than anything he could have bought her. His sacrificial act revealed the depth of his love for her. When so much else was being stripped away from him, his love for my mom remained and compelled him.

We tell that story a lot in our family. It shows the heart of our father.

Love moved the heart of our heavenly Father to act on behalf of His children. He sent His only Son, Jesus Christ, to earth to rescue us in love and by great sacrifice. Great love can be talked about, deep passionate love can be expressed verbally or even written down, but love expressed in action proves that it actually exists. Romans 5:8 says, "But God proves his own love for us in that while we were still sinners, Christ died for us." We know God loves us because of the cross.

Write 1 John 3:16 in the space provided below.

Does this verse mean God is asking us to lay our lives down and die as Jesus did? The answer is no, but let's explore what Jesus did versus what He is asking us to do.

> Jesus didn't commit the ultimate act of love solely for His friends. According to 1 John 2:2, who did Jesus die for?

Jesus died even for those who reject Him.

READ MATTHEW 5:43-46.

> According to this passage, who does Jesus tell us to love?

> Who are your enemies? How can you love them? What would that look like?

God hasn't called all of us to lay down our lives like Christ did in His death, but He has called all of us to lay down our lives daily in service and love, which requires a different kind of death—death to our selfish nature.

When my father walked to the mall and back to attempt to purchase my mom a gift, He did so because he deeply loved his wife. He found joy and pleasure in serving her that way. It's easy to love our family and friends, but loving our enemies or people we don't know is much harder.

> Can you think of a time when God told you to show love to someone you didn't know or perhaps didn't like? Was it hard to do?

In this Advent season, as you reflect and prepare your heart for the remembrance of Jesus' coming to earth to rescue us, ask God to put someone on your heart who you can love through an act of kindness. Maybe that means taking Christmas cookies to a grumpy neighbor or a family member who's hard to love.

When Jesus entered our sin-ridden world and gave His life for us, He demonstrated how vastly He loves us. In the safety and fullness of His love we can love others with action.

One of my favorite stories in the Bible is in Luke 7:36-50. In this passage, Jesus was dining at a Pharisee's home when "a woman in the town who was a sinner" (v. 37) came in and washed Jesus' feet with her tears and her hair. Then she anointed His feet with perfume. About this brave act of love, Jesus said, "Therefore I tell you, her many sins have been forgiven; that's why she loved much. But the one who is forgiven little, loves little" (v. 47). The woman expressed her love for Jesus in a vulnerable and extravagant act. She was able to love much because of the love she had received. We can do the same.

Praise God I have been forgiven much! And out of that forgiveness I can love much. I can express my love for Jesus by loving others with tangible action, and so can you!

What's one action you can take during the Advent season to show someone the love of Jesus?

Write down three names of people in your life who might be changed by a sacrificial act of love. Ask God how you can show them love this season.

Describe a time when someone reached out to you in a way that made you feel loved.

Describe a time when you reached out in love to bless someone in the name of Christ. How did that person react? How did it make you feel?

READ ROMANS 12:9-21.

Meditate on all the ways this passage describes how we can love one another. Think of practical ways you can put this passage into action. Note them below.

Be encouraged that with actions of love, you can overcome evil with good in Jesus' name!

CHRIST'S LOVE COMPELS US

by Chelsea Collins

First, read 2 Corinthians 5:14-21.

There are many roles in our lives that compel us to take action. As wives, we're compelled to serve our husbands (most of the time). As mothers, we're compelled to raise our children in the best environment and care for their every need. As daughters, we want to make our parents proud with our life choices. As friends, we're motivated to be available to those we care about. What's the foundation of these compelling desires? Love. Without love driving us, we're simply fulfilling obligations.

READ 2 CORINTHIANS 5:14-21.

Note the first verb in verse 14. How would you define *compel*?

The Greek verb Paul used here is *synechō*.[4] *Synechō* implies pressure that "confines and restricts as well as controls."[5] Although this seems harsh, in context, it's a call to live anew in light of the fact that Christ died sacrificially for us. Before we can understand what our calling is, we need to understand who we are in Christ.

Once we've accepted Jesus as Savior and Lord of our lives, the Holy Spirit lives in us and we're a new creation. As Paul proclaimed,

> The old has passed away, and see, the new has come!
>
> *2 Corinthians 5:17*

Those who follow Christ are new creations. (See Rom. 6:1-23; Gal. 2:20; Eph. 4:20-23; and Col. 2:13.)

One of my favorite things about winter is the anticipation of spring. In the winter, everything in nature is asleep, but when the weather starts warming up, we begin to see tiny green sprouts, nests with bird eggs, and baby animals. Just as spring weather gives new life to nature, Jesus gives new life to us. We're made new creations by believing in Jesus and living in His sacrificial love demonstrated on the cross.

> List the phrases Paul used in 2 Corinthians 5:16-21 to describe who we are in Christ. Which ones resonate with you? Why?

REREAD VERSES 18-19.

Paul said that Christ's sacrifice for us on the cross has reconciled us to God. We read about this exact moment of reconciliation in Matthew 27:

> But Jesus cried out again with a loud voice and gave up his spirit. Suddenly, the curtain of the sanctuary was torn in two from top to bottom, the earth quaked, and the rocks were split.

Matthew 27:50-51

The curtain in the temple separated the holy of holies, where the presence of God resided, from the rest of the temple. Only the high priest could enter the holy of holies and then only once a year on the day of atonement. When the temple's curtain was torn at the moment of Jesus' death, it signified the direct access all believers in Christ have to God the Father.

What compelled God to send His Son to our broken world as the sacrifice for our sins? The same thing that compels us to sacrifice for our family and friends—love.

> Look up the following verses. According to these passages, why did Jesus die for us?
>
> • John 3:16

- Romans 5:8

- Ephesians 2:4-6

- 1 John 4:9-10

Let's remember that if we've accepted God's gift of salvation, there's nothing that can separate us from His love (Rom. 8:38-39). Be encouraged today that His love for you is unconditional, everlasting, and better than any love you'll experience here on earth.

REREAD 2 CORINTHIANS 5:14,21.

In the beginning of today's study we focused on the word *compel*. Paul said that the love of God compels us. What are you compelled to do because of Christ's love for you and because of your love for Christ?

Before He ascended to heaven, Jesus' last commandment was,

Go, therefore, and make disciples of all nations, baptizing them in the name of the Father and of the Son and of the Holy Spirit, teaching them to observe everything I have commanded you. And remember, I am with you always, to the end of the age.

Matthew 28:19-20

As believers, we're ambassadors for Christ. Therefore, we're called to go and make disciples. As representatives of Christ and living testimonies of how His sacrifice has transformed us, we must be ready to share His truth out of the love we have for Jesus and His people.

Recall the last time you shared the gospel with an unbeliever. Did you feel prepared and eager to share? How did you feel afterward?

How wonderful that we serve a God who loved us enough to send His Son to die for our sins and give us new life.

Close in prayer, thanking God for trusting you to be His ambassador of the gospel. Ask Him for the confidence and boldness to share His story with others.

> [God] made the one who did not know sin to be sin for us,
> so that in him we might become the righteousness of God.
>
> *2 Corinthians 5:21*

DAY 5

THE WONDER OF HIS LOVE

by Savannah Ivey

First, read 1 John 3:1.

Have you ever seen something so striking it left you speechless? Something so beautiful you couldn't shake it from your mind? Maybe you've watched the sun set over the ocean and leave the landscape warm with color. Or maybe you've gazed up at the stars in the night sky that stretched beyond your ability to see. In those moments, we're awestruck by a sense of wonder and mystery, and that wonder can last for years as we think back on the beauty we beheld.

> Can you remember a time when something so beautiful or striking left you speechless? Describe the experience below.

What if we saw Jesus' birth with an even greater sense of wonder? What if we considered not only the mysterious beauty of the Savior coming to the world in the most unlikely way but also the great news our Father delivered to us through Christ's birth—that He loves us so much He sent His Son into our sin-ridden world so we could be reconciled to Him forever?

This sense of wonder at God's love for us is found in 1 John 3:1. The verse opens with the word "See," or as the King James Version translates it, "Behold." Think about the weight of that word, *behold*—doesn't it get your attention? The opening grabs us by the shoulders as if to say, "Stop. Focus. Something big is coming. Get ready."

READ 1 JOHN 3:1 BELOW.

See what great love the Father has given us that we should be
called God's children—and we are!

1 John 3:1a

Perhaps the most wonder-filled truth of all is that God gave us the gift of His
great love. What's more, the NIV says He "lavished" us with His love, meaning
God doesn't hold anything back. He wants us to be part of His family.

Consider what it means to be a child of God. As a child (and even as an
adult) how did your parents or others lavish their love on you?

Now, read what Jesus said about the love of earthly parents:

If you then, who are evil, know how to give good gifts to your
children, how much more will your Father in heaven give good
things to those who ask him.

Matthew 7:11

No matter how loving godly, earthly parents may be, our heavenly Father's love
for us is *even greater.*

Maybe you've thought before about what it means to be a child of God, or
maybe this news is brand new to you. But what if you stopped and considered
the awe-inspiring truth that the Creator of the universe loves you so much that
He went to great lengths to make you His child. Acknowledge the wonderful
truth that, through Jesus, you're called daughter.

Through Jesus—His birth, death, and resurrection—being a child of God isn't
merely a name, because 1 John 3:1 says it's who we are! Because of Jesus, we
don't have to earn our place in God's family. We don't have to talk Him in to
saving us. We don't have to wonder where we belong. We're God's daughters,
and we belong to His family.

God looks beyond our surface and sin to the depths of our souls that long to be children of a perfect, loving, compassionate, faithful Father. He sent His Son to a broken world to claim us as His own, so that we can be called His children. All He asks of us is to behold the truth that through Jesus, we gain the astounding privilege to be His children because He is our infinitely and unimaginably loving Father.

Read Romans 8:14-17. According to this passage, what privileges do we have as children of God? List as many as you can think of.

In his book *Romans 8–16 For You*, Tim Keller shares seven privileges we have as children of God according to Romans 8:14-17. They include:

1. Security in our relationship with our Father (v. 15a);
2. Authority in our status as children (v. 15a);
3. The ability to cry out to God as *Abba*, a term of great intimacy (v. 15b);
4. Assurance, through the Spirit, that we're God's children (v. 16);
5. An inheritance as heirs of God (v. 17);
6. Discipline from a loving Father (v. 17);
7. Family likeness as we share in Christ's sufferings (v. 17).[6]

Which one of these privileges doesn't sound much like a privilege to you? How might your view change if you considered it as proof of your status as God's child?

Jesus is the ultimate gift to us from our loving Father. Like any good gift-giver, our Father is excited for us to receive His gift. Have you ever been so excited to give someone a gift that you could hardly wait for that person to open it? What if that's how God felt about giving us His Son? What if the Creator of the universe excitedly awaited the day He would claim a weary world as His own?

Think back to whatever it was that left you speechless. Now think about the depth of love God showed us through sending His Son and inviting us to be His children. Can you see this love with a new sense of wonder?

Psalm 136 tells us that God's "faithful love endures forever." From the beginning of time to the very end, and even outside of time itself, He has loved us. On that first Christmas, God's love broke through in a gift so grand that we no longer have to search for our identities; our identities are forever established as God's children. Our identities are found in who our Father is—a giver of good gifts to His children—and what Jesus did for us on the cross.

The gift of Jesus isn't only for us to behold; it's for us to share with the world.

> How can you show the love of God to someone this Advent season? Do you have someone in mind who needs to know about the gift of Jesus?

Advent is a season of waiting. Jesus came to earth and will come again to reign forever. And so we wait again. Knowing we're God's children, we can wait well for our Savior who loves us. And when He returns, "we will see him as he is" (1 John 3:2). Can you imagine the great beauty when we behold the wonder of God's love?

In this season of Advent, what will you behold? Amidst the beauty of the holiday found in the lights, decorations, music, and time with loved ones, will you pause and consider the wondrous love the Father has lavished on us?

HOW CAN YOU BE A BEARER OF GOD'S WONDROUS LOVE TO OTHERS?

SPREAD LOVE AND

CHRISTMAS CHEER

by Larissa Arnault Roach

Because God first loved us, we can love others. This week, get out of the house and spread the love of Christ to your family, people in need, and everyone you meet.

First, discover a local organization or ministry where you can volunteer a few hours of your time. Whether it's a local mission, food bank, a coat drive, or people who need assistance paying for heat in the colder months, there's bound to be an organization that could use your time and gifts to serve others.

Second, select two people in your life to receive a letter of gratitude. This could be your spiritual mentor, a loved but far away family member, a teacher or coach from high school—the more (seemingly) random the better! In your letter, tell them specifically why you appreciate them and the difference they have made in your life by being in it. List the positive qualities you see in them that affirm Christ's love shining through their lives. Tell them you love them.

Third, amid the hustle and bustle of the season, choose one person to intentionally spend time with. It might be the new mom you haven't seen in a while, your grandfather in your hometown, or your significant other. Share a meal together one on one, drive around and look at Christmas lights, or bundle up and go for a wintry hike. Talk about the highs and lows of the past year and your hopes for the future.

Pray for other ways to be the hands and feet of Jesus as you encounter people at the coffee shop, around the office, and in the pew next to you at church. Think through the five love languages—acts of service, words of affirmation, quality time, physical touch, and gifts[7]—as you consider all the ways you can show love.

TALK ABOUT
GOD'S LOVE

by Karen Daniel

It's easy to get caught up in the festivities that surround Christmas and forget the true reason we celebrate. Take some time to focus on the gift of God's love with your family this year.

Take a moment and be completely honest as you consider your answer to the following question: Does your excitement about Christmas rest more in God's great love for us or in the cultural entrapments of the holidays?

I'll go first and admit it's really easy for me to get caught up in the distractions that come with this season. Shopping, cooking, shopping again, parties, shopping some more ... my excitement defaults to the cultural stuff. I have to remind myself frequently to keep my focus on the main thing: celebrating the gift God gave us in His Son.

> For God loved the world in this way: He gave his one and only Son, so that everyone who believes in him will not perish but have eternal life.
>
> **John 3:16**

What. A. Gift.

When was the last time you shared with your teen just how much God loves us—that God gave us His Son as an expression of His great love?

A recent study revealed that only 27 percent of teens reported having spiritual conversations in the home.[8] If you're unsure how to engage your teen, Christmas makes an ideal starting point. References to Jesus and God's love for us are all around. They're in the songs we sing at church, on the decorations in our homes and around town, and in just about every greeting, even from strangers, this time of year: Merry Christmas!

As you go about the busyness of this season, take advantage of the "as you go" opportunities in the car or in the Target® aisle to talk with your son or daughter about where they notice God's love being reflected. Remember, you don't need to have all the answers, and there's no right or wrong—just begin with one simple conversation that will hopefully lead to future conversations and a lifetime of talking about God with your family.

If you don't already incorporate Scripture reading and prayer into your family's Christmas Eve or Christmas Day traditions, consider reading the story of Jesus' birth in the Book of Luke as part of your celebration. Then ask this question of each family member, starting with yourself: How do you know God loves you? Close in a time of prayer, thanking God for the wondrous gift of Jesus Christ.

SHOW LOVE TO YOUR
NEIGHBORS

by Bekah Stoneking

Presents in beautiful wrapping paper can seem like one of the most exciting parts of Christmas. Some people love receiving gifts and others love giving gifts. The most amazing gift of all comes to us from the most amazing Giver of all. God loves us with such a great love that He gave us the gift of His Son, Jesus. Jesus came to seek and save the lost—and this includes you and me!

Have you turned from your sins and trusted in Jesus as your Rescuer? If you have, sing a song of praise to God or write a prayer in your journal thanking God for the amazing gift of new life He has given you in Christ. If you haven't yet become a follower of Jesus, talk to your family and to your church leaders about what this means. The gospel is good news for all people and it's a free gift for everyone.

Your challenge is to talk to three Christians this week. Ask them about how they received the gift of salvation and how Jesus has changed their lives.

Then, as a family, practice living like Jesus lived by showing love for God and for your neighbors. Perform acts of service and kindness around your neighborhood. You could help a neighbor shovel their snow or offer to carry in their groceries, or you could bake cookies with your family and use them to fill treat bags for your neighbors and friends. Secretly leave the bags at people's doors with a note reminding them about the love and joy of the Christmas season.

Everywhere you go this week, be on the lookout for a way you can show love to the people around you and remind them of the way God showed His love for us through Jesus.

WRAP-UP

How has your understanding of Advent changed since starting this study?

Which week of study resonated with you most? Why?

After doing this study, how would you answer these questions: Why did Jesus come to the earth? What are we to do in response to His coming?

How can you be a bearer of hope, peace, joy, and love to your community?

Close your time in prayer, thanking God for the gift of Jesus. Pray that you would live in anticipation as you wait on Christ's return, when He will make all things new.

ENDNOTES

WEEK 1

1. John S. Dwight, "O Holy Night!," *Baptist Hymnal* (Nashville, TN: Lifeway Worship, 2008), 194.

2. Priscilla M. Jensen, "The Surprising History of 'O Holy Night,'" The Weekly Standard, December 22, 2017. Available online at www.weeklystandard.com.

3. James Montgomery Boice, *Boice Expositional Commentary – Genesis, Volume 1* (Grand Rapids: Baker Books, 1998), 250.

4. Ibid.

5. Arthur W. Pink, *The Nature of God* (Chicago, Moody, 1999), 61.

6. D. W. Ekstrand, "The Intertestamental Period and Its Significance Upon Christianity," The Transformed Soul. Accessed June 24, 2019. Available online at www.thetransformedsoul.com.

7. "Hanukkah," History, updated September 12, 2018. Available online at www.history.com.

8. John Piper, "God Is Always Doing 10,000 Things in Your Life," Desiring God. January 1, 2013. Available online at www.desiring god.org.

WEEK 2

1. Ibid., Dwight.

2. "*Hamartano*," Strong's G264, Blue Letter Bible. Available online at www.blueletter-bible.org.

3. Dennis Cole and Mark Rooker, "Fellowship Offering from the Flock (3:6–11)," *Leviticus* (Nashville, TN: B&H Publishing Group, 2011).

4. Joseph Mohr and John Freeman Young, "Silent Night, Holy Night," *Baptist Hymnal* (Nashville, TN: Lifeway Worship, 2008), 206.

5. "Introduction to Luke," *Matthew Henry Bible Commentary, Luke 1*. Accessed June 24, 2019. Available online at www.christianity.com.

6. Klyne Snodgrass, *The NIV Application Commentary: Ephesians* (Grand Rapids: Zondervan, 1996), 126.

7. Ibid., 131.

8. Rick Ezell, "Sermon: Being a Peacemaker - Matthew 5," Lifeway. January 01, 2014. Available online at www.lifeway.com.

9. Juliana Menasce Horowitz, "Most U.S. Teens See Anxiety and Depression as a Major Problem Among Their Peers," Pew Research Center. February 20, 2019. Available online at www.pewsocialtrends.org.

10. Ibid.

WEEK 3

1. Ibid., Dwight.

2. C. S. Lewis, *Reflections on the Psalms* (New York: HarperOne, reprint edition 2017), 109.

3. George H. Guthrie, *The NIV Application Commentary: Hebrews* (Grand Rapids: Zondervan, 1998), 195.

4. Ibid, Guthrie, 399.

5. Marshall Segal, "The Joy We Know Only in Suffering," Desiring God. October 18, 2018. Available online at www.desiringgod.org.

6. Elisabeth Elliot, *Keep a Quiet Heart* (Ann Arbor, MI: Servant Publications, 1995), 4.

7. "*Kenoō*," Strong's G2758, Blue Letter Bible. Available online at www.blueletterbible.org.

8. C. S. Lewis, *Mere Christianity* (New York: HarperOne, revised 2015), 50.

9. Ibid., 228.

10. Marie Kondo, *Spark Joy: An Illustrated Master Class on the Art of Organizing and Tidying Up* (Ten Speed Press, 2016).

11. Build a shoebox online for Operation Christmas Child at www.samaritanspurse.org/operation-christmas-child/buildonline.

WEEK 4

1. Ibid, Dwight.

2. Ibid.

3. Jessica Whittemore, as discussed in "Aristotle's Metaphysics: The Four Causes," Chapter 7, Lesson 6. Study.com. Accessed June 26, 2019. Available online at https://study.com.

4. "*Synechō*," Strong's G4912, Blue Letter Bible. Available online at www.blueletterbible.org.

5. Footnote for 2 Corinthians 5:14-15, *The CSB Study Bible for Women* (Nashville: Holman Bible Publishers, 2018), 1479.

6. Summarized from Tim Keller, *Romans 8–16 For You* (UK: The Good Book Company, 2015).

7. Gary D. Chapman, *The 5 Love Languages: The Secret to Love that Lasts* (Chicago: Northfield Publishing, 2015).

8. Ben Trueblood, *Within Reach: The Power of Small Changes in Keeping Students Connected* (Nashville, TN: Lifeway Press, 2019), 38.

EMILY CHADWELL

Emily Chadwell is married to Seth, the absolute love of her life. Together they have a sweet little girl named Claire and an active Golden Retriever named Hampton. When Emily isn't spending time with her family, she serves as an editor at Lifeway.

PAIGE CLAYTON

Paige Clayton manages the Adult Live Events area for Lifeway. Prior to her work at Lifeway, Paige worked for the Operation Christmas Child project with Samaritan's Purse. She is currently finishing up a master's in Professional Counseling. In her spare time, she is a fun aunt to four young adult nieces and mom to her dog, Ruby. She loves traveling to places she has never been, singing, and spending time outdoors and with her family.

CHELSEA COLLINS

Chelsea is the editor for *Lifeway Mujeres* and works with Hispanic women all over the world to create content for women. She and her husband, Chris, have been married for three years and live in Smyrna, Tennessee, with their two fur babies, Marlee and Nala. Chelsea earned a bachelor's degree from Union University in Spanish and loves that she is able use it every day. She enjoys afternoon naps, cross-stitching, and traveling whenever she can.

KAREN DANIEL

During the week Karen Daniel serves as the publishing team leader of Lifeway Student Ministry. The rest of the time she and her husband, Brian, can be found volunteering at Grace Church in Hendersonville, Tennessee, visiting their two daughters in Washington, D.C., and Knoxville, or perhaps in Rupp Arena cheering on their beloved Kentucky Wildcats.

LEIGH ANN DANS

Leigh Ann Dans is a graphic designer for the marketing area of Lifeway Women's Bible studies and events. She's mother to a wonderful daughter, Christina, and grandmother to two grandchildren, Kayden and Macayla. Leigh Ann is an outside girl, who loves to meet with Jesus while they walk and talk together out under the sunshine and trees.

DEBBIE DICKERSON

Debbie Dickerson and husband, Steve, love spending time with their oldest son, Landon, and his wife, Alyssa, and their college-aged son, Kaden. Debbie enjoys serving as editor of *Mature Living* and as a children's teacher at ClearView Baptist Church in Franklin, Tennessee.

SARAH DOSS

Sarah Doss is a content and production editor with Lifeway's Adult Ministry team. With an educational background in Communications from the University of Georgia, Sarah is currently pursuing an M.A. in Christian Studies from Southeastern Baptist Theological Seminary. In her spare time, Sarah enjoys watching quirky sitcoms, a strong cup of coffee, and travel (international or otherwise). She calls Nashville, Tennessee, home. Keep up with her on Twitter® @sarahdossy.

RACHEL FORREST

Rachel Forrest is a ministry wife and mom of two (ages six and four). She lives in Oklahoma and serves as the women's ministry leader in her church where her husband is on staff as the bivocational worship minister. She has an M.A. in Theological Studies and works as a developer for B&H Academic Digital, a subsidiary of Lifeway Christian Resources. She prefers to spend her days potting plants, reading a good book on her patio, or running. You can connect with her through social media on Twitter and Instagram® @r8chelforrest.

ASHLEY MARIVITTORI GORMAN

Ashley Marivittori Gorman serves as the women's publisher at B&H Publishing Group, an imprint of Lifeway Christian Resources. She is currently completing her MDiv from Southeastern Theological Seminary and has also been trained under The Charles Simeon Trust. Her passions are biblical literacy, discipleship, foster care, theology, and books. Ashley and her husband, Cole, live in Nashville, Tennessee, with their daughter Charlie. You can follow her on Twitter or on Instagram @AshMarvGorman.

MICHELLE R. HICKS

Michelle R. Hicks is the manager for Women, Marriage & Family resources at Lifeway Christian Resources. Michelle served as a freelance writer, campus minister, and corporate chaplain before coming to Lifeway. She is a graduate of the University of North Texas and Southwestern Baptist Theological Seminary. Michelle has a deep hunger for God's Word and wants others to discover the abundant life they can have with Jesus as their Lord and Savior.

ELIZABETH HYNDMAN

Elizabeth Hyndman reads, writes, and debates the nuances of punctuation. Officially, she's a content editor at Lifeway. She managed to find a job where she uses both her English undergraduate and her seminary graduate degrees every day. Elizabeth grew up in Nashville, sips chai lattes every chance she can get, and believes everyone should have a "funny picture" pose at the ready. Follow her on Twitter or Instagram @edhyndman.

SAVANNAH IVEY

Savannah Ivey served as the event project coordinator for Women's Leadership Training Events at Lifeway. She is originally from Knoxville, Tennessee, and is a graduate of the University of Tennessee, where she studied Communication and Psychology. Her background is in student and women's ministry, and she is passionate about helping women know and love the real, living Jesus. She loves conversations with friends, road trips, coffee, and music.

CONTRIBUTORS

KELLY D. KING

Kelly D. King is the manager of Magazine and Devotional Publishing and Women's Ministry Training for Lifeway Christian Resources. She holds a Master of Theology from Gateway Seminary. She has more than thirty years of leadership experience, both as a lay leader in the local church and in vocational ministry. She is married to Vic, and they enjoy summers in Colorado and time with their family in Oklahoma.

BETSY LANGMADE

Betsy Langmade builds, plans, and coordinates events for Lifeway Women around the country. She's a mom and grandmother to her growing family and has been married to David for forty-three years. When she's not traveling or working, she enjoys her downtime outside and making memories with the family.

CONNIA NELSON

Connia Nelson is a ministry, business, and customer-focused leader who has held a number of key positions in the corporate, community, and church environments. In her current role at Lifeway as the chief human resources officer, Connia is a transformational HR leader, trusted advisor, and change agent. Connia currently leads a woman's community group at Rolling Hills Community Church in Franklin, Tennessee, where she is also a member of the finance committee.

MICKEY PITTS

Mickey Pitts serves as the strategic partnership and solutions manager at Lifeway Christian Resources, which is a fancy way of saying she gets to make friends and investigate new tools to serve the body of Christ! Mickey loves ministering to women and coaches women's Bible study leaders in her local church. Mickey and her husband, Reed, live in Spring Hill, Tennessee, with her eight-year-old stepson, Landon, and a crazy Wheaten Terrier named Dexter.

LARISSA ARNAULT ROACH

Larissa Arnault Roach is the marketing team leader for Lifeway Women. She loves butter, books, and bright lipstick. Always up for a good party—Christmas or otherwise—she considers Ecclesiastes 2:24-25 her life verses. Larissa lives in downtown Nashville with her husband, Nate, two kids, and Margot the sweet, but wild, Brittany.

RACHEL SHAVER

Rachel Shaver is a book marketer for B&H Publishing Group by day, and by night, a mom to three sweet, rowdy kids. She affectionately refers to them as the "toddler mafia." She and her husband, Evan, make their home in a little town right outside Nashville, Tennessee.

CONTRIBUTORS

AMANDA MAE STEELE

Amanda Mae Steele is a writer and photographer with a background in film and musical theater. After moving to Nashville, Tennessee, from Los Angeles with her husband, Nick, and sweet puppy, Dino, Amanda Mae landed at Lifeway on the Creative Media Production Team, where she loves serving her team of ten creative guys. She is passionate about women's ministry, learning about other cultures, and ice cream.

BEKAH STONEKING

Bekah Stoneking serves as content editor for *Explore the Bible: Kids* at Lifeway Christian Resources, where she develops worship curriculum and resources for preschoolers and kids. She holds a Master of Arts from Southeastern Baptist Theological Seminary and is a Doctor of Education candidate, also at SEBTS. She lives in Nashville, Tennessee, where she enjoys spending time with her church family and teaching first and second graders at The Church at Avenue South.

MARY MARGARET WEST

Mary Margaret West serves as the girls ministry specialist for Lifeway, which basically means that teenage girls and the women who lead them are her favorite people on the planet. Mary Margaret is the author of *Show Her the Way: Your Guide to Discipling Teen Girls*, is a former girls minister, and holds a master's degree from New Orleans Baptist Theological Seminary. Mary Margaret is married to Jonathan. Together, they love living in Franklin, Tennessee.

MARY C. WILEY

Mary C. Wiley lives with her husband and two children in Lebanon, Tennessee. She gets to work with words everyday as the marketing strategist for women's books at B&H Publishing Group at Lifeway. Mary is pursuing a Master of Arts in Theological Studies and hosts the Questions Kids Ask Podcast. Read more from Mary at marycwiley.com or @marycwiley, and be on the look out for *Everyday Theology*, an 8-session Bible study on what we believe, why we believe it, and how it transforms every aspect of our lives.

EMMA WILSON

Emma Wilson is the digital and social media strategist for Lifeway Women. She and her husband, Garrett, said "I do" in December 2018, and they have served in YoungLife together ever since they met as leaders in college. Emma is an Alabama native with a city girl's heart and loves exploring her home in Nashville, Tennessee. A perfect day looks like coffee shop hopping, perusing local bookstores, cooking something from scratch, and sharing it all with friends. You can follow her online at emmacaitlyn.com.

JESSICA YENTZER

Jessica Yentzer is a marketing strategist on Lifeway's Adult Ministry team. Well-written memoirs, dark chocolate, a good running trail, and the perfect fall day are just a few of the things that put a smile on her face. When she's not planning marketing strategy, she loves hiking and exploring the outdoors with her husband, Grant.

LIGHT A CANDLE

In the Christian tradition, many light a candle each week of Advent. You may have seen this take place in churches around the world. We light the candles during Advent to represent the Light who has come into the world, Jesus (Isa. 9:6). As we mark each week leading up to Advent, we also consider the themes that surround the season, all of which we root in Jesus' coming to earth—hope, peace, joy, and love. If you would like to participate in this tradition in your home, we've provided a quick guide for you below.

Week 1: Hope

As you light the candle this week, prayerfully consider the hope God brings to the world and read the following passage.

> The people walking in darkness have seen a great light; a light has dawned on those living in the land of darkness.

> **Isaiah 9:2**

Week 2: Peace

As you light the candle this week, prayerfully consider God's peace coming into our hearts and minds and the peace Jesus brings between us and God. Then read the following passage.

> For a child will be born for us, a son will be given to us, and the government will be on his shoulders. He will be named Wonderful Counselor, Mighty God, Eternal Father, Prince of Peace.

> **Isaiah 9:6**

Week 3: Joy

As you light the candle this week, meditate on the incomparable joy that we can know in God alone and read the following passage.

> After seeing them, they reported the message they were told about this child, and all who heard it were amazed at what the shepherds said to them.

> **Luke 2:17-18**

Week 4: Love

As you light the candle this week, meditate on God's unconditional love for us all year long by reading the following passage.

> For God loved the world in this way: He gave his one and only Son, so that everyone who believes in him will not perish but have eternal life. For God did not send his Son into the world to condemn the world, but to save the world through him.

> **John 3:16-17**

BECOMING A CHRISTIAN

Romans 10:17 says, "So faith comes from what is heard, and what is heard comes through the message about Christ."

Maybe you've stumbled across new information in this study. Or maybe you've attended church all your life, but something you read here struck you differently than it ever has before. If you have never accepted Christ but would like to, read on to discover how you can become a Christian.

Your heart tends to run from God and rebel against Him. The Bible calls this *sin*. Romans 3:23 says, "For all have sinned and fall short of the glory of God."

Yet God loves you and wants to save you from sin, to offer you a new life of hope. John 10:10b says, "I have come so that they may have life and have it in abundance."

To give you this gift of salvation, God made a way through His Son, Jesus Christ. Romans 5:8 says, "But God proves his own love for us in that while we were still sinners, Christ died for us."

You receive this gift by faith alone. Ephesians 2:8-9 says, "For you are saved by grace through faith, and this not from yourselves; it is God's gift—not from works, so that no one can boast."

Faith is a decision of your heart demonstrated by the actions of your life. Romans 10:9 says, "If you confess with your mouth, 'Jesus is Lord,' and believe in your heart that God raised him from the dead, you will be saved."

If you trust that Jesus died for your sins and want to receive new life through Him, pray a prayer similar to the following to express your repentance and faith in Him:

"DEAR GOD, I KNOW I AM A SINNER. I BELIEVE JESUS DIED TO FORGIVE ME OF MY SINS. I ACCEPT YOUR OFFER OF ETERNAL LIFE. THANK YOU FOR FORGIVING ME OF ALL MY SINS. THANK YOU FOR MY NEW LIFE. FROM THIS DAY FORWARD, I WILL CHOOSE TO FOLLOW YOU."

If you have trusted Jesus for salvation, please share your decision with your group leader or another Christian friend. If you are not already attending church, find one in which you can worship and grow in your faith. Following Christ's example, ask to be baptized as a public expression of your faith.

LET'S BE FRIENDS!

BLOG

We're here to help you grow in your faith, develop as a leader, and find encouragement as you go.

lifewaywomen.com

SOCIAL

Find inspiration in the in-between moments of life.

@lifeaywomen

NEWSLETTER

Be the first to hear about new studies, events, giveaways, and more by signing up.

lifeway.com/womensnews

APP

Download the Lifeway Women app for Bible study plans, online study groups, a prayer wall, and more!

 Google Play   App Store

Lifeway women